QUOTABLE
NOTRE DAME

QUOTABLE
NOTRE DAME

Edited by
Jim Langford and Jill Langford

QUOTABLE NOTRE DAME

10 9 8 7 6 5 4 3 2 1

ISBN 9780982784686

Library of Congress Control Number 2011921569

Cover photo: Don Nelson

Published by
Corby Books
A Division of Corby Publishing LP
P.O. Box 93
Notre Dame, Indiana 46556
(574) 784-3482
www.corbypublishing.com

Manufactured in the United States of America

*To Jeremy, Joshua, Trevor and Emily Langford
and all who honor Notre Dame
in their heart and life*

TABLE OF CONTENTS

PROLOGUE

A prayer attributed to Mother Teresa

People are often unreasonable, illogical and self-centered
   Forgive them anyway.
If you are kind, people may accuse you of selfish, ulterior
motives
   Be kind anyway.
If you are successful, you will win some false friends and
some true enemies
   Succeed anyway.
If you are honest and frank, people may cheat you.
   Be honest and frank anyway.
What you spend years building, someone could destroy
overnight.
   Build anyway.
If you find serenity and happiness, people may be jealous.
   Be happy anyway.
The good you do today, people will forget tomorrow.
   Do good anyway.
Give the world the best you have, and it may never be
enough.
   Give the world the best you've got anyway.
You see, in the final analysis. It's between you and God
   It never was between you and them anyway.

PREFACE

It goes without saying that attempting to select essential quotes from the storied life of the University of Notre Dame is likely to be a fool's errand. How does one choose from the rich records of this history and spirit? Should the selection be limited to one liners or should it include some that require a story to provide context for the content? We elected to do some of both.

Rather than succumb to paralysis in the face of so much material, we chose quotes and stories that seemed to us to capture those elements that combine to display the splendor of this place and its people.

To be sure, there are entries that describe toil and tragedy, but even they evoke responses that say something about the spirit that lives and grows at Notre Dame. Some of the quotes are multiple entries from the same individual persons. For us the deciding factor was whether particular quotes or observations conveyed better than others an aspect of the whole story we want this book to tell.

We are grateful to Eileen Carroll for the excellent design and production of this book, and to all who, in those cases where permission seemed required, allowed us to include their material.

Our hope is that this book will provide both pleasure and inspiration.

JimLangford
Jill Langford

First College Building – circa 1843

HISTORY

"To have a history is to have a name, and the richer the history the more glorious the name."

– Fr. Thomas McAvoy, C.S.C.

"Because of a lack of funds Father Sorin had almost never left France. Providentially, a woman in LeMans donated a gold chain which was raffled off, and with this unexpected money, Sorin and six religious brothers sailed from Le Havre."

– Professor Edward Fischer

On August 8, 1841, Father Edward Sorin and six brothers of the Congregation of Holy Cross, none of whom spoke English, set sail from Le Havre, France, aboard an overcrowded passenger ship named the *Iowa*. Sorin had been ordained in 1838 and was now 27 years old.

From the moment he set sail until he died at Notre Dame on October 31, 1893, he never stopped moving in the service of God, Country and Notre Dame. Given land in northern Indiana by the Bishop of Vincennes, Sorin and his companions made their way north.

Letter of Father Edward Sorin to Father Basil Moreau, Founder of the Congregation of Holy Cross, December 5, 1842:

"Beloved Father:

"When we least dreamed of it, we were offered an excellent piece of property, about 640 acres in extent. The land is located in the county of St. Joseph, not far from the city of St. Joseph (Michigan). It is a delightfully quiet place, about twenty minutes from South Bend. This attractive spot has taken from the lake that surrounds it the beautiful name of Notre Dame du Lac...It is from here that I write you now.

"Everything was frozen over. Yet it all seemed so beautiful. The lake, especially, with its broad carpet of dazzling white snow, quite naturally reminded us of the spotless purity of our august

Lady whose name it bears, and also of the purity of soul that should mark the new inhabitants of this chosen spot. ...We were in a hurry to enjoy all the scenery along the lake shore of which we had heard so much. Though it was quite cold, we went to the very end of the lake, and like children, came back fascinated with the marvelous beauties of our new home. ...Once more we felt that Providence had been good to us and we blessed God from the depths of our soul.

"Will you permit me, dear Father, to share with you a preoccupation which gives me no rest? Briefly, it is this: Notre Dame du Lac was given to us by the bishop only on condition that we establish here a college at the earliest opportunity. As there is no other school within more than a hundred miles, this college cannot fail to succeed. ...Before long, it will develop on a large scale ...It will be one of the most powerful means of good in this country.

"Finally, dear Father, you cannot help but see that this new branch of your family is destined to grow under the protection of Our Lady of the Lake and of St. Joseph. At least, this is my deep conviction. Time will tell if I am wrong.

E. Sorin

Though certified by the State of Indiana as a university in 1844, early Notre Dame was a university in name only. It encompassed religious novitiates, preparatory and grade schools and a manual labor school, but its classical collegiate curriculum never attracted more than a dozen students a year in the early decades:

"No young man or boy was turned away who wished to attend Notre Dame, and who could, by one means or another (cash, labor, barter) pay some sort of tuition for his support. There were no entrance requirements and students were simply placed wherever they seemed to fit into the curriculum."

– Historian Thomas Schlereth

Courses in physics and geology were added to the curriculum in 1863, and two years later the College of Science was established. In 1869 the University established the nation's first Catholic law school, and in 1873 the first Catholic College of Engineering. Its architecture program also was the first in the U.S. under Catholic auspices, and its circulating library was the first on any American campus.

By the eve of the Civil War, the student population at Notre Dame had risen to over 200, mostly from Midwest states. Still, some of the older students left to join in the fighting. In the course of the war, seven priests from the C.S.C. community joined to be chaplains, the most famous of whom were Fathers Peter Cooney and William Corby. More than 60 Sisters of the Holy Cross joined the effort as nurses. Though a teaching order, their Civil War work extended their work to heath care, a ministry they still preserve to this day.

At the Battle of Stones River, Tennessee, in December of 1842, Father Cooney earned this praise from the Commander of the 35th Indiana:

"To Father Cooney, our chaplain, too much praise cannot be given. Indifferent as to himself, he was deeply solicitous for the temporal and spiritual welfare of us all. On the field he was cool and indifferent to danger and in the name of the regiment, I thank him for his kindness and laborious attention to the dead and dying."

Memorable too are the tributes to Father Corby, chaplain of the famed Irish Brigade, who distinguished himself throughout his years of service, but is best remembered for the general absolution he gave to the troops of the Brigade at Gettysburg:

"Father Corby approached Colonel Patrick Kelly, now in charge, saying to him, 'For two or three weeks we have been marching constantly. My men have not had a chance to get to confession. I must give them one last bit of spiritual comfort. Let me stand up on this rock where all may see me. Let me speak to them.' It was so ordered. Above the terrible din of battle Father Corby told the men that since it was impossible at the moment to hear the confession of the Catholic boys, they could be restored to the state of grace by prayerfully receiving the general absolution that he was about to impart. Let them, in their hearts, make a firm act of contrition and a resolution to embrace the first opportunity of confession. As he finished these few words, and placed the purple stole over his shoulders, every man, Catholic and non-Catholic, fell to his knees. The chaplain's hand was raised in absolution. Immediately thereafter the officers shouted 'Order Arms!' The troops wheeled and rushed down into the alley to repulse the Confederates. For a moment Corby stood motionless on the rock. He was gazing on the back of many a soldier running to battle in his grave clothes.

"The scene was more than impressive; it was awe inspiring."

– Major St. Clair Mulholland of the 116th Pennsylvania

That moment is forever captured in the statue of Father Corby at the battlefield in Gettysburg, a replica of which stands in front of Corby Hall on the Notre Dame campus.

Years later, Father Corby (who went on to serve two times as President of Notre Dame and Provincial of the Holy Cross Province) recalled:

"My eye covered thousands of officers and men. The situation really reminded me of the day of judgment...so great were the whirlwinds of war then in motion."

Upon Fr. Corby's death, December 28, 1897, a veterans' group ordered a headstone bearing these words:

"He was a noble soldier, ever ready at the call of his office to perform the duties of the Chaplain; fearless under every trial of life. Whether as a soldier in behalf of his country, or as a soldier of the cross, he has ever been ready to lift up the fallen, support the weak and sustain the strong."

Let it be noted and remembered that the brave service of Holy Cross priests, brothers and nuns did a great deal to combat the anti-Catholic sentiment that was common in those days and, sadly, for years to come.

Growth of the student and faculty population was modest but steady over the decade or so following the Civil War. By 1879, there were 34 faculty members and nearly 400 students. But tragedy and trial would come soon enough:

"The morning of April 23, 1879, was refreshing. There was sun enough to be pleasantly warm. And from the lake to the west, a slight breeze was blowing. And it was Wednesday, a free day for the students. Just a few days previous, Father Sorin had packed his bags for another trip to Europe. He would go by way of Montreal and embark from New York some ten days later. He had made a point of informing the community that he disliked these frequent jaunts abroad. And on this lazy April day, so dangerously close to spring fever epidemic, the air was unexpectedly rent with the sudden, shrill cry that rose from the voices of Minims [children in the trade school]—they were the first to see it—'Fire, fire! The college is on fire!' It was eleven o'clock.

"The flames were low on the college roof, close to the little railing that ran around the dome. Workmen had been on the roof as late as ten o'clock making some repairs. At that hour they had descended, locking the door behind them. If, when the fire was first detected, water in any quantity could have been brought to the roof, it would have been easily extinguished. But the building was six storeys high; the buckets placed for just such an emergency were empty; and in the confusion that ensued precious time was lost. In ten or fifteen minutes the pitch roof began to blaze, sending forth clouds of dense smoke.

"Water, by steam pressure, was finally forced into great tanks on the roof. Everyone who could help rushed to form the lines of a bucket-brigade, but soon the water in the tanks was exhausted. Some heroic souls, panting and shouting, stayed on the roof, hoping against hope that the fire might be crushed out. But when the supports of the dome burned away, and the statue went crashing below in a billow of sparks and flame, even the most courageous thought only of saving whatever effects might be carried out of the burning building."

– Fr. Arthur Hope, C.S.C.

"Time marked its ceaseless course through the terrible burning even as it had done in the hours of peace, study and prayer. We shall never forget that bell, unruffled and peaceful, as it was heard, and barely heard, amid the crackling and roaring of the flames, the falling of walls, the noise of the engines, the rushing and hissing of water and the loud shouts of men—the peaceful but appalling sound of those sweet church bells striking the hours of God's ever passing time, His quiet, all-embracing eternity."

– Scholastic, June, 1879

"Many in and around South Bend showed a good will that was immediate and practical. There had been no dinner that day, of course, and although the fire had not penetrated to the kitchens, the good Sisters were swamped with anxiety and work. Many South Bend residents brought food and the offer of shelter. For the most part, however, they were able to make only passable adjustment for the night.

"Luckily the weather was balmy and the students manifested great good will in supporting the inconveniences caused by the fire. What students remained on the grounds found shelter in Washington Hall. Bedding and pillows were spread out on the floor. The stage was occupied by the faculty. In the midst of disaster, a good-natured sense of humor expressed itself when the students, looking about at their unaccustomed plight, began singing, 'The old home ain't what it used to be!' Of course, it was a heavy night for Father Corby. His most anxious thought was: 'How will this affect Father Sorin?' And it was a matter of no small concern. Father Sorin was no longer a young man. It was feared that news of Notre Dame's disaster would be too great a shock for him. They determined, therefore, to notify the superior at St. Laurent College, Montreal, asking him to keep the news from Father General until a messenger could arrive from Notre Dame. That night, at nine o'clock, trusty Jimmy Edwards took the train to Montreal to break the sad news to Father Sorin personally.

"… It was a terrible blow, for in three hours was wiped out the result of thirty-five years of hard, grueling sacrifice. It took something more than courage to face the future. Father Corby had promised the students a new Notre Dame by September. But as the ashes began to cool, he himself wondered if he had not been too optimistic. How would Father Sorin feel about it?

"A few days later, he found out. The sixty-five-year-old man walked around the ruins, and those who followed him were confounded by his attitude. Instead of bending, he stiffened. There was on his face a look of grim determination. He signaled all of them to go into the church with him."

– Father Arthur Hope, C.S.C.

Faculty member Professor Timothy Howard recorded what followed:

"I was then present when Father Sorin, after looking over the destruction of his life-work, stood on the altar steps of the only building left, and spoke to the community what I have always felt to be the most sublime words I ever listened to. There was absolute faith, confidence, resolution in his very look and pose. 'If it were ALL gone, I should not give up!' were his closing words. The effect was electric. It was the crowning moment of his life. A sad company had gone into the church that day. They were all simple Christian heroes as they came out. There was never more a shadow of a doubt as to the future of Notre Dame."

– Timothy Howard

"More than any other single event or quote in the history of Notre Dame, the spirit evidenced by Father Sorin on that day embodies for me the spirit that has never left the campus. It is a large, founding part of what makes the place a field of grace."

– Jim Langford

The rebuilding began almost immediately.

"There was not a cart, wheelbarrow or wagon that was not impressed into service. Every member of the community felt it his duty to don old clothes and show how he could labor. Even some students, in a burst of enthusiasm, insisted that they, too, would stay on and do what they could. Bright and early on April 30th, the students got a wheelbarrow and began work—loading up bricks which their Latin professor was to haul away. The work was hard, their enthusiasm waned, and the next morning, they could not be found."

– Fr. Arthur J. Hope, C.S.C.

"Ground was broken on Saturday, May 19; the first stone was placed on Monday, May 21. It was estimated that 4,350,000 bricks were going into the new building... It was an architectural marathon... By September the College building was finished and ready."

– Fr. Arthur Hope, C.S.C.

In 1880, the statue of Mary atop the Dome was donated by the women of St. Mary's.

"The glistening dome in the light of the orb of day presents a most brilliant spectacle to the travelers on our railroads as they draw near to South Bend, and to the observer elsewhere for miles around."

– Aug. 14, 1886 Scholastic

In fact, it became the world's best-known symbol for a university.

·"If the edifice stands, we will never regret the price and sweat that it has cost us."

– Rev. Edward Sorin, C.S.C.

"The number and spirit of the pupils in the college seems to be improving upon preceding years ... God grant that His Kingdom be sought first and always and by each and every one, and that we may thus deserve the continuance of the blessings without which we can do nothing."

– Fr. Edward Sorin, C.S.C.

"Sorin had the vision and reflexes of an artist, and he is still here. He lives on in the lives of each of us who is willing to put up a fight, no matter what the odds, for this very special place dedicated to the Mother of God."

– Professor Robert Leader

"I despise the many who worship success and who are ever ready to censure failure. Failure, when not the result of culpable imprudence, obtains my sympathy, and the effort that proceeded it, my approval. The safe conservatism which never moves lest it fail, I abhor: it is the dry-rot in the Church, and my heart goes out to the man who never tolerated it in his calculations. Safe conservatism would have left the Apostles in Palestine."

– Archbishop John Ireland in a sermon
at Notre Dame, August, 1888

"It is better to have a small attendance at the University with good discipline than a large attendance without it."

– Fr. Thomas E. Walsh, C.S.C.,
President of Notre Dame in 1890

"But more important by far than buildings is the proper preparation of our young subjects for their work as teachers. What every university needs and what every community needs, above everything else, is scholars and specialists, as well as devoted religious. Large and imposing buildings have little value unless those in charge of them and teaching in them be thoroughly educated and properly trained to teach the special classes which may be assigned to them."

– Fr. John Zahm, C.S.C. to Matthew Schumacher C.S.C.,
Director of Studies, August 30, 1913

"Like all the oldest buildings at Notre Dame, Sacred Heart is built of yellow clay bricks, formed from the very mud of St. Mary's Lake. The central pillars encase the trunks of enormous hardwood trees that also came from the university's grounds. Using these local materials, Father Sorin and his religious confreres deliberately set about the task of recreating the ancient Gothic traditions of Catholic Europe in the new circumstances of nineteenth-century America. Once again the architectural plan has something very deliberate to say. The University of Notre Dame is self-consciously Roman Catholic in its identity and design. The Main Church stands directly next to the Main Building with its famous Golden Dome. At Notre Dame, therefore, faith and reason stand side by side, at the very heart of the campus. From this central axis, the University extends down Notre Dame Avenue and outward toward the wider world it was founded to serve and educate."

– Former Rector of Sacred Heart Basilica, now Bishop of Peoria, IL, Daniel Jenky, C.S.C.

"The campus includes more than a square mile of park, and students are expected to take their recreation on the campus rather than loitering about the city. College life lasts only four years as a rule and the special charm of it lies in the points wherein it differs from the life of the city rather than in the points wherein it resembles that life. These are the years when young men dream dreams and see visions."

– Notre Dame Catalog, 1915

"His [Sorin's] deep piety and faith were combined with traits that now seem very American. He took chances, he tried much and failed often, he fought and won and fought and lost, but he never lost his drive and his optimism."

– Tom Stritch

Part of the celebration of the Golden Jubilee of Father Sorin's ordination was a talk by Father John Zahm, who noted:

"It is because he has been able to communicate his enthusiasm to others and carry along with them that he has been able to accomplish what otherwise would have been simply impossible.

18

It is because he has always retained his youthful ardors; because he has always been buoyed up by a hope that has never faltered; because he has known how to surmount the many obstacles that obstructed his path; because he has been able to overcome the opposition that would restrain his high aspirations that he is today able to contemplate...what can be accomplished by one who, like our venerable founder, has placed his faith and confidence in God and in the Queen of Heaven whom he always so faithfully and chivalrously served."

"Sorin's shadow still hangs over Notre Dame, above all in the place itself. The campus is uniquely beautiful, especially the old parts that Sorin personally designed, whether he had an architect or not. Much of it recalls Sorin's memories of his native Sarthe Department in France, just north of the valley of the Loire. But the spacing of the old buildings, and the planting in the main quad, largely Sorin's work, is superb. Few American colleges can rival its layout, none its trees. Many besides Sorin and Hesburgh have loved the place, but none has left a mark on it so powerful and inimitable as theirs."

— *Tom Stritch*

"Fr. Sorin hardly qualifies as a great educational theorist or intellectual. He was neither a regular teacher nor a serious scholar. He contributed relatively little to discussions regarding curriculum at Notre Dame as it slowly evolved into a genuine institution of higher learning. Fr. Sorin, instead, was an ambitious institution builder and a decisive leader. His courage and iron will insured that Notre Dame survived and eventually prospered despite fires, a cholera outbreak, and a series of financial crises. Yet Fr. Sorin was much more than this. He was a man of deep faith who believed that God and Our Lady had summoned him across the Atlantic Ocean to undertake a crucial work in Catholic education.

"From the outset, Fr. Sorin hoped that Notre Dame would develop as a 'most powerful means for good' by preparing young Catholics to go forth and serve well in the world. He understood that Catholic education was not only about training minds but also about forming character and shaping souls. While no great educational theorist, he assuredly got to the heart of the matter."

– Fr. Wilson D. Miscamble, C.S.C.

"One of the surest and safest means to prevent the collapse of society is to bind and to hold more and more strongly bound the child's heart to the parent's heart, to the family, to home, to primitive and innocent affections."

– Fr. Edward Sorin, C.S.C.

"One of the most famous foods served to students in the 1920s was the 'Notre Dame bun.' Former Professor Richard Sullivan describes the buns as 'inexpressively excellent when fresh and piled with unsalted butter; but hardening gradually as they aged down the week, until they petrified finally into legend, and became formidable to dental fillings, and were universally cursed and celebrated, and addressed in ink and plastered with a stamp and mailed—bare parcel post— to friends, parents, sweethearts, all over the country.' "

– Cited by T. Schlereth

"Great abilities, unless supported by virtues, are in danger, and seldom prove a blessing."

– Fr. Edward Sorin, C.S.C.

"Education, in its proper sense, implies the expansion and cultivation of all the faculties, mental and physical—the cultivation of the heart as well as the mind; and of these the formation and enrichment of the heart is undoubtedly the most important of the two."

– Fr. Edward Sorin, C.S.C.

"My great and ever-growing ambition is now to finish the work I have commenced or continued, that, when I disappear, it may remain and go on increasing and developing for the glory of God and the salvation of souls."

– Fr. Edward Sorin, C.S.C.

"On St. Edward's Day, October 13th, the students and faculty knew that all was not well. For the first time in all those years, Sorin was unable to attend the celebration. He was so unwell that he could not even go to the college parlor. In his own rooms in the presbytery, however, he received delegations of students and faculty.

The congratulations were mercifully short. He thanked them in a subdued voice and his great frame, trembling and shaking, followed them to the porch. The band was gathered there, and when Sorin appeared, they broke loose. He smiled and waved his hand gently to them, then turned, and with some assistance, re-entered the room that was to be his death-chamber. ...

"In the sick room, the bystanders noticed that now and then Father Sorin's face was lighted with a tender smile. At a quarter to ten he slowly opened his eyes and gazed at the religious kneeling about him. It was the only farewell he could make. Then, gently closing his eyes, he expired without the slightest movement or struggle. It was October 31, 1893."

— *Fr. Arthur Hope, C.S.C.*

As the University grew in the first few decades of the twentieth century, it did so in the number of buildings on campus, the number and quality of students and faculty, and in ever-increasing academic standards. The latter was achieved in part by bringing to campus world renowned scholars, writers and lecturers. Perhaps none was as colorful and well-attended as Gilbert Keith Chesterton, whose series of thirty-six lectures drew an average crowd of 500 each. The witty, urbane writer-philosopher enjoyed his time at Notre Dame and its combination of its academic ambition, its football fame and its spiritual life. He wrote a poem dedicated to the University:

"I have seen, where a strange country
  Opened its secret plains above me,
  One great golden dome stands lonely
    with its
  Golden image, one
  Seen afar, in strange fulfillment,
  Through the sunlit Indiana summer,
  That Apocalyptic portent that has clothed
    her with the Sun."

"The boys shout 'Notre Dame' as they watch the fortunes of the fray and Chesterton sees Our Lady presiding fittingly even over a football contest:"

"And I saw them shock the whirlwind
  Of the world of dust and dazzle:
  And thrice they stamped, a thunderclap;
    and thrice the sand-wheel swirled:
  And thrice they cried like thunderclap
  On our Lady of the Victories,
  The Mother of the Master of the Masterers
    of the world."

"He recurs to a favorite thought that the Mother of Sorrows is the cause of human joy:"

"Queen of Death and deadly weeping
Those about to live salute thee,
Youth untroubled; youth untortured;
    hateless war and harmless mirth
And the New Lord's larger largesse
Holier bread and happier circus,
Since the Queen of Sevenfold Sorrow has
    brought: joy upon the earth."

– G.K. Chesterton,
introduced and cited by Maisie Ward

"In his years as President of the University of Notre Dame, Father Hesburgh has spoken more consistently and more effectively in support of the rights of human beings than any American I know."

– President Jimmy Carter,
Commencement speech 1977

Even in the early years of its history, Notre Dame scored a significant number of firsts:

In 1869, Notre Dame established the nation's first Catholic law school; four years later, the first Catholic college of engineering, to be followed shortly by the first Catholic program of architecture.

In 1881, Notre Dame lit the grounds of campus with arc lights and, four years later, it was the first American college to have electric lights.

In 1889, Sorin Hall became Catholic higher education's first student residence with private rooms and the beginning of a residence hall tradition that today houses 80% of the undergraduate students.

In 1899, Dr. Jerome Green, Professor of electrical engineering, was the first American to send a wireless message.

"However you measure it, we here commit ourselves to the something more, not in a triumphant spirit of being superior, but with the humble realization that we must be ourselves at Notre Dame, in keeping with our tradition and that, hopefully, being ourselves will mean that we may add something to the total strength of what we most cherish; the great endeavor of the higher learning in our beloved America and in our total world. How more splendidly can we be a splendid place?"

– Fr. Theodore Hesburgh, C.S.C.

"My first time to ever see Notre Dame was to come here as a sports announcer only two years out of college to broadcast a football game. You won or I wouldn't have mentioned that. ...

"I hope when you leave this campus you will do so with a feeling of obligation to this, your alma mater. She will need your help and support in the years to come. If ever the great independent colleges and universities like Notre Dame give way to and are replaced by tax-supported institutions, the struggle to preserve academic freedom will have been lost."

– President Ronald Reagan,
Commencement speech, 1981

" 'There is no loyalty stronger than the patriotism of a Notre Dame student. There is no conception of duty higher than that which a Notre Dame man holds for his religion or his university. I know that if tonight any of the property of the university or any of its privileges were threatened, and I should call upon you, you would rise to a man to protect it. It is with the same loyalty to Notre Dame that I appeal to you to show your respect for South Bend and the authority of the city by dispersing.' – *Rev. Matthew Walsh, C.S.C., President of Notre Dame, in his attempt to avoid further confrontation between the students and the Ku Klux Klan who convened in South Bend with the intention of burning a cross at Notre Dame. May, 1924.* The weekend of May 17 began with word that mobs of Klansmen were pouring into South Bend."

– Fr. Arthur Hope, C.S.C.

Fr. Hope reconstructs the scene that followed:

"Every street-car, every bus, every interurban vomited forth its strangers, each carrying under his arm a suspicious bundle. The students of Notre Dame were the first to greet them. With a smile, they would touch the descending resident of Goshen or New Carlisle, and ask, 'Are you from the Klan? Have you come for the parade? This way, please!' Up an alley, down a side street, through a dark entrance, and a Klansman would emerge without his sheet, and sometimes with a black eye. For the students it was glorious adventure. They had the time of their lives. Forming a flying wedge, they would advance on a white-clad figure that was directing traffic, and then he was there no longer."

– Fr. Arthur Hope, C.S.C.

But on that Monday, the troubles grew more dangerous. Klansmen armed with clubs and bottles escalated the danger. Father O'Donnell urged the students to assemble at the courthouse in South Bend and Father Walsh convinced them to return to campus, thus averting a violent battle.

It is well known that the United States Navy, by selecting Notre Dame as a training site for midshipmen during World War II, saved the University from the distinct possibility of closing. A high percentage of young men were being drafted into the war effort and a lack of students would require extreme measures by the University. Notre Dame hosted Naval training with gratitude and zeal.

On May 6, 1946, Admiral Chester Nimitz, the leader of America's victory at sea, responded to an honorary degree from Notre Dame by saying:

"Father O'Donnell, you sent forth to me, as to every other naval commands on every ocean and continent, men who had become imbued with more than the mechanical knowledge of warfare. Somehow, in the crowded hours of their preparation for the grim business of war, they had absorbed not only Notre Dame's traditional fighting spirit, but the spiritual strength, too, that this University imparts to all, regardless of creed, who come under its influence."

– Cited by Arthur Hope, C.S.C.

One of the great characters in Notre Dame's history was Fr. Bernard H.B. Lange, C.S.C. Father Lange, once the fourth strongest man in the world, was in charge of the only weightlifting facility on campus, a small gym with a swimming pool, located north of the Main Building. He ruled his domain like a Prussian Field Marshall; if you dropped a weight, whether you were a student or a football player, you would be shown the door. One account has it that:

"His reputation as a non-conformist and superman dates to his years in Notre Dame Preparatory School. It was probably born the day he climbed to the top of the Golden Dome, wrapped his right arm around Our Lady, and waved to his awestruck classmates on the ground far below. The police were summoned and he led them on a frantic chase through St. Ed's Hall and down to St. Mary's Lake, where he made good his escape by swimming under the ice to the far shore, where he broke from the lake headfirst and disappeared into the woods."

– *Dr. Paul Gill*

Father Lange had a sign in front of his gym that said "PRIVATE. STAY OUT." Every summer, the curious students, mostly nuns, would peek in and be rewarded with choice words from the gymmeister. On one occasion, a few timid female graduate students (they might have been nuns) walked in and inquired if they had found the mosquito genetics laboratory, which was next door. "Do I look like a goddam mosquito?" replied the strong man.

To those who worked out under his supervision, Fr. Lange was a great and good man. If there were a Characters Hall of Fame at Notre Dame, Fr. Lange would be a prime candidate.

"If your heart does belong to this place and it still skips a beat when you fly home and see the Dome out the window of the plane, then you need, every now and then, to take a walk between the lakes, past Columba Hall, through the woods, to the community cemetery. It is a veritable small Normandy, all the crosses are the same size; there is Father Sorin, a cross no bigger than the rest; all the names are of now-silent heroes. You will find markers for some who built this place, many who taught and administered here, perhaps some who taught you or were your

32

colleagues. It is their legacy we carry. It reminds us to pay homage to all who labored here before us. I like to imagine that at the moment time turns into eternity, everyone who ever shared the mission of this place will be allowed to turn and give a final salute to Notre Dame. It would surely be a salute that would sweep away the stars."

– Jim Langford

"All the advantages of convenience, attractive scenery, pure and invigorating air, and excellent springs, combine here to form not only a healthful abode, but also an agreeable solitude, which facilitates so effectively the intellectual improvement of youth."

– Notre Dame newspaper ad in 1843

"During the nineteenth and early twentieth century, Notre Dame offered (in addition to the collegiate curriculum) elementary and high school programs as well as a vocational institute, called 'The Manual Labor Training School.' Some campus leaders, like Fr. Andrew Morrissey, president from 1893-1906, defended such pre-collegiate activities and opposed University growth, because he did not think Notre Dame 'could compete with all those schools so heavily endowed.' Others like Fr. John Zahm, provincial of the Holy Cross order from 1898-1906 and the first scientist of note on the Notre Dame faculty, challenged the idea that the non-collegiate program should receive emphasis. He wanted Notre Dame to become 'the intellectual center of the American West.'"

– Robert Schmuhl

Zahm won.
Under President Fr. James Burns, C.S.C., 1919-1922, the academic foundations for a true university were set in place and Notre Dame as we know it, was firmly founded.

"It's no great secret how to become a great university if you can get the resources for it. You have to have an intellectually curious student body, an intellectually competent faculty, and classrooms, laboratories, museums and libraries where they can get together. But a great Catholic university goes beyond that. We need people who have a commitment to the philosophical and theological implications of all the great questions of our times. We need people who inquire about transcendentals and not just temporary things. We need people who are concerned with the moral and the spiritual as well as the intellectual formation of students. You have to have people who can speak to values and whose life professes them. Such teachers are rare, and that is why becoming a great university is easy compared to becoming a great Catholic university."

– Fr. Theodore M. Hesburgh, C.S.C.,
quoted by Robert Schmuhl

"What made the Notre Dame story so compelling in the 1920s wasn't just that they had Rockne, Gipp and the Four Horsemen, or that they kept winning games and collecting national titles—but that they were, openly and proudly, Catholic, and that their rise to prominence coincided with the rise of Catholics into the American middle class. They became the 'us' in the great 'us versus them' battle that American Catholics waged with the Protestant establishment and every time they beat a school like Princeton, they struck a blow for the cause. Al Smith might lose the election, but Notre Dame won the game. Anti-Catholic prejudice was still widespread in America in the 1920s and Notre Dame became one of the chief weapons against it. When the Ku Klux Klan staged a big march in South Bend in 1924, Notre Dame students went downtown to fight them; the Notre Dame football team fought a wider foe on an even larger field. Rockne's players upended the ugly caricature of Catholics that many Americans held—strange, Latin-mumbling Old World relics beholden to Rome—and showed that theirs was a religion not just for frail old women in veils, but also for burly young men in shoulder pads."

– Kevin Coyne

"As I settled into my new office and position, I evolved a goal for myself. What did I want to accomplish for Notre Dame? The answer came silently as a kind of vision. I envisioned Notre Dame as a great Catholic university, the greatest in the world! There were many distinguished universities in our country and in Europe, but not since the Middle Ages had there been a great Catholic university. The road was wide open for Notre Dame, I told myself. ...

"My new deans [one of Fr. Hesburgh's first moves was to appoint five new Deans] all had two things in common: they had high aspirations for Notre Dame and they had the ability to lead. John Cavanaugh used to say that leadership was a very simple matter. All you needed was a vision of where you wanted to go and the ability to inspire a lot of people to help you get there."

– Fr. Theodore Hesburgh, C.S.C.

"There will come times in the lives of all of us, when we'll be faced with causes bigger than ourselves and they won't be on a playing field. If they want to see the goodness and love of life of this generation, the commitment to decency and a better future, let them come here to Notre Dame."

– President Ronald Reagan

It was World War II and its aftermath that changed Notre Dame forever. New residence halls, more students, more scholars—all might have never have happened had the United States Navy not selected Notre Dame as a place to educate and train its midshipmen during the War. From 1942 to 1946, 11,925 Navy men completed their officers training at Notre Dame and, in addition, several thousand more Navy and Marine trainees were here for part of their training for combat. Upon war's end, many who had sampled Notre Dame life now returned to complete their college education on the G.I. bill. A veritable town, Vetville, sprung up to house married vets and their families. Recruiting of faculty, including European scholars fleeing Communism, was markedly successful. Enlarging and upgrading the Graduate School while still preserving the quality of undergraduate education became a reality. Under Fr. John J. Cavanaugh, C.S.C., as President, and Fr. Theodore Hesburgh, C.S.C., as Executive Vice President, a whole new thrust toward excellence began in earnest. And never stopped. Fund raising to support excellence became formalized under Jim Frick. In 1952, Fr. Hesburgh was named President. A new Notre Dame was here to stay.

Father Charles O'Donnell, C.S.C., President and poet of Notre Dame, wrote of the campus:

"So well I love these woods I half believe
There is an intimate fellowship we share;
So many years we breathed the same brave
     air,
Kept spring in common, and were one to
     grieve
Summer's undoing, saw the fall bereave
Us both of beauty, together learned to bear
The weight of winter—when I go other
     where—
An unreturning journey—I would leave
Some whisper of a song in these old oaks,
A footfall lingering till some distant summer
Another singer down these paths may
     stray—
The destined one a golden future cloaks—
And he may love them, too, this graced
     newcomer,
And may remember that I passed this way."

"I don't believe the world needs another Duke or Northwestern. It does need a Notre Dame that's great in its own way."

— *Professor Larry Cunningham*

"Notre Dame is a wonderful place to work, which is not to say perfect. Unlike some of my experiences in the private sector, nearly everyone really wants to be here and shares allegiance to the basic tenets of the mission. They also tend to be friendly, generous people. At one of the commencement ceremonies last year, a departing senior said it well: 'The Notre Dame experience—from the outside looking in, you can't understand it; from the inside looking out, you can't explain it.' "

— *Matt Storin, former Editor of the* Boston Globe

(He retired as associate vice president for news and information in January 2006. He continues to teach at the University.)

"...History is not a record of all that happened, but only all that happened that someone thought worth preserving with some kind of record in writing, photograph, oral tradition or whatever ways and means. The miracle of Notre Dame, as the miracle of the Church, might well be simply its survival and flourishing."

– Fr. Nicholas Ayo, C.S.C.

Campus View – circa 1856

ACADEMICS

"I try to teach not just what they need to know, but to light a fire in the gut."

— *Fr. Wilson Miscamble, C.S.C.*

"He was a saintly man. That is what I sensed as I scuffled through the leaves on my way back from Maritain's last lecture at Moreau (1958). He loved the truth, but his purpose in life was not to win arguments. He wanted to be wise, such an odd combination for a philosopher! He succeeded because he prayed as hard as he studied."

— *Professor Ralph McInerny*

"Good teaching is a sort of sacramental action, a communication of spirit."

— *Fr. John W. Cavanaugh, C.S.C.*

"Being at a Catholic university does not shield one from the full range of human types, fancies and foibles. There are no guarantees that some in the community will not miss the point of its being Catholic on the one hand or a university on the other...St. Thomas Aquinas, challenged for his use of the pagan Aristotle's philosophy, replied, 'Take the truth no matter where you find it.' I cherish working at Notre Dame in part because here we do not need to be afraid of the truth or of where it leads us."

– Jim Langford, Director Emeritus, University of Notre Dame Press

"Openness to dialogue is one of the best aspects of academic study...it is no use for me to speak peace—to claim that I honor difference—while waging war on everyone who disagrees with me. Honest intellectual give and take can provide a model of some utility not only for our relations with one another, but also for what a living faith might look like."

– Notre Dame theologian Blake Leyerle

"Teaching is finally far more about creating a space in which education can happen than about throwing information to students like fodder. This sounds very therapeutic, but I casually learned it from Aristotle who commented that while beginning students can reel off the words they have heard, for real education to occur, 'that subject must grow to be part of them, and that takes time.' For knowledge to be real it must be lived, incorporated into the stuff of one's life."

– ND Kaneb Teaching Award winner,
ND Theologian Blake Leyerle

"...(Y)ou have come here to this place of Notre Dame, this great and dominant Catholic university of the United States, a place concerned through all the years with integrating a true faith and a true philosophy with the life of culture. In your time here, you must have become better aware of the composition of life, of the nature of true primacy. You must have considered here and found here the answer to 'the old question which traverses the sky of the soul perpetually, the vast, the general question, what is the meaning of life?' If you are convinced of your answer, you will not be deluded by the lies and phrases;

you will be able to resist the pressure of the age. Possessed as you should be of a true spiritual culture, you will not be too much disconcerted or ravaged by contemporary civilization; you will not feel yourselves prisoners of life, scratching on the walls of your cells; you will not succumb to the sorrows of the savage world. Instead, you will save yourselves and save all those who encounter you in your various works and ways and vocations."

– Frank O'Malley, Summer
Commencement Address, 1956

"I appreciate the presence, beauty and hope of your lives. These are the last words you will hear from me—for the time being anyway. I don't know what's in store for me in the near future or the far-off future. And I hope you'll remember these words. I have a wish and hope for you. I hope that time will never trap you, and that the world will have time for you. I hope that you will be happy forever and that you recollect the happiness of human existence which is sometimes sorrow and suffering, and sometimes love. My love to you! Peace and thanks."

– Frank O'Malley in one of his last classes
at Notre Dame, 1973 (from notes of Gary Caruso)

"The best teachers that I had at Notre Dame had one thing in common: a certain inner strength that came, perhaps, from a sense of vocation. Each seemed to be doing what he was meant to do; each was absorbed in his work and did not seem to be glancing around to see what 'good deal' might beckon from afar.

"By the way they gave a shape to their courses they brought assurances to those of us who were unsure. Instead of a labyrinth they offered a direction. We were spared the uneasy feeling that our teachers were 'just winging it.' We sensed that they knew where they were taking us and that we would arrive at our destination in good time."

– Edward Fischer

"If one Notre Dame professor from the twentieth century is remembered a thousand years from now, it will be Ivan Mestrovic...Whenever I enter the old studio, by way of the Snite Museum of Art, I picture the Master seated beneath the northwest window. The room recalls for me how strongly he held the old-fashioned belief in work and workmanship, an attitude that reflects a certain order of the soul.

"Once you see such grace, the awareness always haunts you. And it serves as an uneasy measure of your own vocation."

– Edward Fischer

"I have always disliked teaching that gets down on all fours with the students. Good teaching is sort of like naval gunfire: you need a little distance for your shots to take effect."

– Tom Stritch

"Hesburgh inherited a college which had just turned the corner to university status. He left it a full-fledged university on its way to the top. Hesburgh's own prestige advanced with Notre Dame's. Notre Dame, already well known for its football splendors, gradually became known for its academic ones...There had been vision and promise before Hesburgh. But now the circumstances were ripe. By 1952 Notre Dame was ready and Hesburgh was its prophet."

– Tom Stritch

"Teaching is a moral activity. 'My colleagues and I,' he [Professor Stephen Rodgers] said, 'had to be examples for our students as our teachers had been for us, and their teachers for them, back as long as there have been people willing to learn and people presumptuous enough to try to teach them. We cannot help it.'"

– *Edward Fischer*

"I encourage my students to really interrogate their relationship with the media-saturated world that surrounds them," he says. "When you introduce different ways of looking critically at what seems so familiar, a kind of pedagogical spontaneous combustion can occur—and it's those golden moments that are the most rewarding. I have no interest at all in simply downloading information."

– *ND Professor Jim Collins, Sheedy Award 2010*

"Every professor who sticks in my memory had a way of endowing things with importance, an importance that was there all along but needed to be brought to the surface so that the rest of us might see. That is the art of teaching."

– Edward Fischer

"[Professor] Withey, like all good teachers, was uneasy in the presence of banality...he felt that at any given time the university should be the mountain peak of a culture where the best of the past is cherished and the best of the present is encouraged. Out of that belief teachers can give students a vision of life well-lived, where the first-rate is cherished above the third-rate. In this environment the young evolving out of darkness may begin to care about a life of the mind. Some may even realize that it can be exhilarating."

– Edward Fischer

"I love to see in our Notre Dame of today the promise of the potency of a Padua or a Bologna, a Bonn or a Heidelberg, an Oxford or a Cambridge, a Salamanca or a Valladolid. It may be that this view will be regarded as proceeding from my own enthusiasm, but it matters not. I consider it a compliment to be called an enthusiast. Turn over the pages of history and you will find that all those who have left a name and a fame have been enthusiasts, and it is because our venerable Founder [Father Sorin] has been an enthusiast—I use the word in its primary significance—that he has been able to achieve so much."

– Fr. John Zahm, C.S.C. on the
Golden Jubilee of Fr. Sorin in 1888

(It was Father Zahm who worked tirelessly to change Notre Dame from a manual trade school orientation to that of a real university.)

"It is one of the great temptations of the modern academy to stand on the sidelines of history satisfied with occasional ironic utterances or glib putdowns directed at the power brokers of the political, economic and social spheres. A much better alternative is to try to produce thoughtful leaders, informed prophetic voices, and people of integrity and good sense."

– Edward A. Malloy, C.S.C.

"Certainly, the building of respect doesn't mean that we'll always agree with each other, but it does make it more likely that we'll communicate with each other. Sometimes, the open and plentiful exchange of our disagreements makes it look like we don't have our act together. That's true: With God's help we're still writing the script and rehearsing our parts, so don't expect perfection. More importantly, I think Notre Dame can be proud of the dynamic marketplace of ideas that exists on campus and of the outpouring of interest that we generate throughout the American public when a controversy erupts here."

– Rev. John I. Jenkins, C.S.C., President

"At a Catholic university we have a special challenge to make sure that the door between the life of the mind and the life of the spirit is kept wide open. In our tradition of faith seeking understanding, it is essential that we be engaged in and wholeheartedly committed to the creative process. We cannot simply be reactionary bystanders or critical commentators. We must reverse a cultural condition in which caution squelches intellectual curiosity."

– Former Notre Dame Provost Timothy O'Meara

"I realize there are some great forces at the heart of this place that daily feed my soul. One is the campus I walk on that fills itself up with the breathtaking beauty of all four seasons, each lending a change of landscape colors to buildings of all sizes, shapes, and vintage positioned along many paths. One young man visiting campus caught the power of it all when he remarked to another, 'Just walking across this campus makes me want to get inside one of these buildings and study something.'"

– Jean Lenz, O.S.F.

"No matter what the mood of the hour, the University stands as a witness to the unseen; a sensitivity to 'beyondness' saturates these acres. The spirit is still held in high regard here.

"Because of an alertness to the transcendent, Notre Dame has never lost its sense of mystery. It never tried to fool students into believing that knowledge solves mysteries to a real depth. In the community cemetery are men who realized that a real education increases an awareness of mystery and develops a sense of wonder.

"Since a spirit of religion persists, it has always been easy to say yes to life at Notre

Dame. While this place has known its cynics, it never developed a milieu in which cynicism was in and optimism was out. An affirmation of life is not considered corny on this campus. Perhaps that is why a blessing still lies upon the place."

– Edward Fischer

" 'Wisdom does not come from knowledge only. Its other parent is love. And its gift is action in a common cause much larger than self.' That sounds like our own Father Theodore Hesburgh. His mark is on this campus, this country and this world."

– Jim Langford

"The student must be made to realize that his great achievement is not the discovery of something new to him, but the finding of a law, a principle, a compound or a species hitherto unknown or unrealized by the world."

– Fr. Julius Niewland, C.S.C.

FACTS: The Notre Dame *Scholastic* (Originally *The Scholastic Year*) was founded in 1867; *The Dome* was first published in 1906. The Notre Dame Law School, the nation's oldest Catholic law school, opened in 1869. Between 1942 and 1946, the number of Navy personnel who completed officers' training at Notre Dame was 11,925.

"I am a strong believer in having the kind of faculty in which every individual professor excels as a teacher of undergraduates, as a teacher of graduate students, and as a scholar and researcher."

– *Former Provost Timothy O'Meara*

"Education is the great problem of the age.... None but an educated people can be a permanently free people."

– *Orestes Brownson*

"Father Hesburgh emphasizes that leadership involves articulating a vision and getting others to own it as their own, especially colleagues:

'The secret is really to get the very best people you can get, even if they are better than you are, and to get them in the right slot. But once you get them appointed to that slot and get their agreement to do the work, then leave them alone. Don't try to second-guess them. Don't try to say who is going to be their assistant and who is going to work with them. That's their problem. I always told them: "You do your work and I'll do mine. Whatever you do, you're going to get the credit for it, and whatever you do I'll back you on it. Unless you make an absolute mess of it, I'm with you all the way." As a result, people know that they have their own bailiwick that they are going to run themselves. They are going to pick their people and they are going to have a reasonable freedom to have their own particular vision within the larger vision....Administrators who don't make it are fussy administrators who are constantly sticking their noses into other people's business and telling them how to do things. A much better system is to get people who know much more about a specific area than you do and let them go.' "

– *Father Hesburgh, quoted by Professor Robert Schmuhl (1986)*

"There's a certain excitement at Notre Dame at this time. It is the excitement of being part of an institution which not only makes promises about excellence, but seems capable of mastering the will and the resources...to enable the realization of those promises."

– North Central Association accreditation evaluators in 1984, cited by Robert Schmuhl

"Notre Dame is a unique environment in that it provides an excellent education for its students, research opportunities for its faculty, and a commitment to values which benefits the entire community."

– Emeritus Professor J. Kerry Thomas

"I find the sense of loyalty and pride at Notre Dame delightfully refreshing in an increasingly cynical world."

– Emeritus Professor Michael J. Etzel

"In its 150 years of existence, the University of Notre Dame has grown from a grade school parading as a University to an undergraduate college with a few advanced programs to its present status as a nationally renowned university with increasingly high aspirations in graduate education and research....

"Peace, ecumenism, world development, the world Church: it's a large stage on which we have chosen to play, but frankly we feel we have a unique opportunity to occupy a significant role in the great dialogues of our time. Our rapid growth has positioned us for this role, our academic strength qualifies us for it, and our tradition of faith gives us a distinctive voice with which to speak. And so we shall."

– *Edward A. Malloy, C.S.C., President, 1992*

"There is certainly a different spirit at Notre Dame—sort of an inspiration that causes faculty to do more—to do better. I know that some faculty would say that they wouldn't have the same emotional involvement at another university that they have here. Here they're willing to sacrifice. They stayed here through periods when our salaries were low and they could have gone to other places. They are willing to take on extra loads and extra assignments because they really believe in the place. They feel it's a place worth building, preserving and making outstanding, and they're proud of it."

– Former Engineering Dean and Associate Provost Roger A. Schmitz

And what of today? Some headlines:

~ Notre Dame Research Awards Exceed $100 Million

~ Improving Global Health

~ Notre Dame faculty receive two $100,000 Grand Challenges Explorations grants from the Bill & Melinda Gates Foundation to explore bold and largely unproven ways to improve health in developing countries

~ Young Alumna Awarded for Aiding Farm Workers

~ The Mendoza College of Business at Notre Dame has been selected as a winner of a 2010 Brillante Award for Excellence in recognition of its work to support the educational advancement and recognition of Hispanic Americans and Hispanic communities across the nation.

~ A renowned scholar, devoted educator, caring physician, and compassionate humanitarian, *Dr. Stacy Rudnicki '78*, recently was invested as the inaugural recipient of the Kathryn and J. Thomas May Professorship in Neurology/ALS at University of Arkansas for Medical Sciences (UAMS)

And the beat goes on....

Notre Dame's esteemed Rev. Louis Putz, C.S.C., an unselfish giver throughout his entire adult life, once said that life consists of three stages: learning, earning, and returning.

"The goal of a university is not to amass a lot of money. It's not to build a large endowment. It's to continually improve in quality, consistent with its mission and its vision. Notre Dame academically has probably never been stronger overall. The academic profile of the students entering the

University—grades in high school, number of AP classes, SAT scores—has never been higher. Extracurricular involvement has never been broader. Our impact, I think, on the world is growing year by year. We now are among the best universities in the country. I would argue that, as a Catholic university, we are a preeminent Catholic university. Maybe the preeminent Catholic university. But we can be a lot better than we are."

– Provost Thomas Burish

"A very good teaching college can help people learn. It can help them discover. But at a research university our commitment also includes teaching those who will teach others to discover. It is to educate the lawyers, the business leaders, the faculty for the future. In the process of providing graduate education, you provide additional opportunities for the undergraduates as well."

– Provost Thomas Burish

"Notre Dame has to stay Notre Dame. It cannot try to emulate or become a secular institution. It can't be driven by rankings. It can't simply try to be preeminent without holding on to its distinctive character. It has to be wholly, proudly, inspiringly Notre Dame. In the area of academics, it must improve or it will fall. If it doesn't improve, we will not be able to recruit students and tell them honestly that they'll get a first-class education. And the last thing we want is to recruit students and not provide them a first-class education so they can compete with anyone."

– Provost Thomas Burish

"It won't be easy, though, to realize these goals, to fulfill the vision for Notre Dame to have the greatest possible influence on the world. But we need to do all we can to continue the momentum of our predecessors and to strengthen even further Notre Dame's academic excellence, the quality of its teaching, its research and discovery. We have wonderful students and a superb faculty and we simply must invest all we can to achieve our goals."

– Rev. John I. Jenkins, C.S.C., President

"At a Catholic University we have a special challenge to make sure the door between the life of the mind and the life of the spirit is kept wide open."

– Former Provost, Timothy O'Meara

"Our mission is to be a law school that is concerned with moral values. It's a place of mixing faith and reason. The values of the Catholic intellectual tradition are our guidepost. We are a national leader not in spite of our Catholic nature but because of it."

– David Link, former Dean of the
Notre Dame College of Law

"Where others see incompatible aspirations, we see creative tensions. We want to be a place that educates students to be influential and accomplished leaders in their chosen field, and to be humble and generous servants to those in need. We want to be a place where faculty are at the leading edge in inquiry and scholarship, and dedicated and effective teachers of our students. We want to be a diverse place and to be a place

65

of community and solidarity. We want to be a university in South Bend, Indiana, and to be a gathering place that is aware of and open to the world. We want to be counted among the best universities in the land, and to be a place of faith with a distinctive Catholic mission. We want to be a place of generous sacrifice, and a place of celebration."

– Rev. John I. Jenkins, C.S.C.,
President, University of Notre Dame

"A look at today and tomorrow for the University of Notre Dame must take into full account the specific promise and challenges we face as we try to create here a great Catholic university. Also, we cannot avoid facing frankly the dangers and difficulties that confront us along the road of present and future development. But neither should we be timid, unimaginative, or defensive. In fact, what we need most at this juncture of our history are of the pioneer: vision, courage, confidence, a great hope inspired by faith and ever revivified by love and dedication."

– Fr. Theodore Hesburgh, C.S.C.,
President Emeritus

"A great Catholic university must begin by being a great university that is also Catholic."

– Fr. Theodore Hesburgh, C.S.C.

"In a setting like Notre Dame we might aspire to connect learning with the pursuit of the Christian life itself. We may not always do that in a conscious fashion, but it is a goal towards which we should strive. What is important is that a place like Notre Dame provides the home where such an exercise of joining life to learning is possible, even if we fail to exercise that possibility to the fullest."

– Professor Lawrence Cunningham,
Notre Dame

"The ability of a Catholic institution to provide perspective and a larger context to the work that is carried on within its confines is a strength not a weakness."

– Professor William Gray

"...Father Sorin had a dream and began a journey to build a great Catholic university. As visionary and wise as he was, it is doubtful he could have envisioned the strength and quality of the Notre Dame of today, not to mention the many different kinds of individuals who study and work here. Be that as it may, it is clear that Father Sorin succeeded magnificently with his segment of the journey or process of building a great Catholic university. Let us not be afraid to add to that journey by using our gifts of faith and intellect to discern the changes of the future and to provide for them. For in fact, each perspective, and each of us who holds it, is equally important in this journey."

– Professor Naomi Meara, Notre Dame

"If Notre Dame pursues its course with integrity, we may be surprised at the friends and admirers in other institutions and sectors of society who cheer for us because they recognize the importance of our venture and the need for a renewed participation in this nation's public and intellectual discourse."

– Fr. Wilson Miscamble, C.S.C.,
Notre Dame

"...I wish to stress the importance of...the vision and determination of those who together make up the Notre Dame community. There exists no unseen force in the world, not even the much-celebrated (and, according to some, inexorable) power of secularization, that can thwart the active and determined collaboration of members of the Notre Dame community to cooperate energetically with the Spirit to realize Father Sorin's dream for Notre Dame: a university at once profoundly Catholic and unsurpassed in scholarship. To this task we consecrate our lives."

– Rev. Timothy Scully, C.S.C., Notre Dame

"I should like for a Catholic university to be as unapologetically Catholic as it is warmly ecumenical; as proudly intellectual as it is caring and compassionate; as concerned with the individual and communal life of the mind as it is with publications; as valuing of inference, imagination and assent as ways to God, as of social justice; as committed to liberal education as it is to professional education; as eager in the pursuit of truth and of Catholic culture in the arts as it is of moral goodness; as steady in its own convictions and traditions as it is appreciative of diversity; as humbled and gratified by the spiritual work of mercy that is rendered in instructing the ignorant as by the corporal mercy performed in sheltering the homeless. The noble activity of cultivating the life of the mind is the first, though not the only, profession and praxis of a Catholic university; that very cultivation is its first and best service to the church, the academy, and the world."

– Professor Emeritus Mary Catherine Tillman,
Notre Dame

"To know something is not simply to mimic the truth but to be able to give reasons and arguments for that truth. This level of reflection ensures that the student will be able to defend a view against the arguments of future opponents instead of just succumbing to their persuasive rhetoric, will be ready to apply knowledge in changing circumstances, and will be equipped to build on existing knowledge and extend it—via the same principles of searching inquiry and rational reflection—into new areas."

– Professor Mark Roche, Notre Dame

"When I was an undergraduate at Notre Dame, Fr. Hesburgh spoke of the Catholic university as being both a lighthouse and a crossroads. As a lighthouse, we strive to stand apart and be different, illuminating issues with the moral and spiritual wisdom of the Catholic tradition. Yet, we must also be a crossroads through which pass people of many different perspectives, backgrounds, faiths, and cultures. At this crossroads, we must be a place where people of good will are received with charity, are able to speak, be heard, and engage in responsible and reasoned dialogue."

– Fr. John I. Jenkins, C.S.C.,
President, Notre Dame

UNIVERSITY REGULATIONS.

SPECIAL RULES.

1. The Students of Notre Dame should at all times and everywhere behave like gentlemen. Therefore, good habits, gentlemanly deportment, politeness, neatness, order, application, respect for God and attention to religious duties are expected from them.

2. All the Students are required to attend the exercises of public worship with punctuality and decorum. They must be provided with books suitable for divine worship.

3. As soon as the bell announces the beginning or end of a College exercise, every one shall repair in silence to the discharge of that duty to which he is called.

4. The time of recreation excepted, silence must be inviolably observed in all places.

5. Students must show themselves obedient and respectful towards the Professors and Prefects of the Institution. They must never absent themselves from the place in which they ought to be, unless with permission from proper authority.

6. Students must carefully avoid every expression in the least injurious to Religion, their Professors, Prefects or fellow-Students.

7. Students are not permitted to visit private rooms.

8. Intoxicating liquors are absolutely prohibited.

9. **Compensation for all damage done to the furniture, or other property of the College, will be required from the person or persons causing such damage.**

10. No branch of study, once commenced shall be discontinued without permission of the Director of Studies.

11. Unless with parents and guardians, Students are not allowed to remain with visitors.

12. No one shall leave the University grounds without permission from the President, Vice-President or Prefect of Discipline.

13. Any breach of pure morals, either in word or action, must be reported forthwith to the President, Vice-President or Prefect of Discipline.

14. Students are not allowed to enter the playgrounds of the other departments without special permission.

15. No students are permitted to take private walks unless accompanied by a Prefect.

16. No one shall keep in his possession any money except what he receives weekly from the Treasurer, on Wednesdays, at nine o'clock, a. m. The College will not be responsible for any valuables, such as watches, money, etc., unless deposited with the Secretary.

17. Bulletins are sent to parents every month.

18. Bath-rooms, provided with hot and cold water, are fitted up for the use of the Students.

19. Stationery, etc., will be delivered to the Students daily, during the morning and the evening recess.

20. Students of low and vicious habits will not be retained in the College.

21. Students who have failed to give satisfaction in the class-room, or who shall have been guilty of misconduct or breach of rule, will be sent to the detention-room during the recreations or promenades, and required to prepare their lessons or perform such tasks as shall be assigned them, and will be excluded from all College exercises until such tasks be accomplished.

22. Every month the Students must write to their parents or guardians. All letters sent or received may be opened by the President, Vice-President or Prefect of Discipline.

23. No book, periodical or newspaper shall be introduced into the College without being previously examined and approved of by the Director of Studies. Objectional reading-matter found in the possession of Students will either be destroyed or withheld from them until their departure from the University.

24. Whether in class or in recreation, when permitted to converse at table, or during their walks, students should endeavor to improve the purity of their language and cultivate urbanity of manners. Bad habits and manners are sufficient to deprive a Student of Degrees and Honors.

25. The Students are reviewed on Wednesdays and Sundays with regard to their personal neatness.

W. CORBY, C. S. C., President.

Student Rules – circa 1866-1872

STUDENT LIFE

"In the winter of 1880, the students in the refectory at Notre Dame were complimented on their courteous behavior. One might gather from this that the table manners of the boys of Notre Dame were quite exceptional. It is difficult to believe, however. For years it had been the practice to have reading at meals. Students were supposed to listen, and sometimes they were questioned regarding the substance of what was being read. Perhaps that practice did help some, but it sorely tried the patience of the boys. Moreover, it occasioned many things not sanctioned in any book of etiquette. During reading it was always funnier to spill gravy in your neighbor's lap, slip a frankfurter into his pocket, or let a platter crash to the floor. Father Corby decided to omit a great deal of the reading at meals."

– Fr. Arthur Hope, C.S.C.

Walter O'Keefe was a student at Notre Dame in the early 1920s. He was a personality, to say the least:

"When O'Keefe was living in Sorin Hall, the prefect of discipline laid down the law at the close of evening prayers in chapel: 'I wish you fellows had more imagination! It gets tiresome hearing the same lame excuses over and over. If when you get into trouble you could give me a fresh alibi, one I have never heard, I might let you off the hook.'

"O'Keefe was already in trouble. Because of a transgression he was campused, meaning he could not go south of Cedar Grove Cemetery until next semester. But a dance band was playing in South Bend, one that he just had to hear. Temptation triumphed and Walter was caught coming out of the Oliver Hotel.

"When appearing before the prefect of discipline the next morning, he said, 'Father, you told us that if someone gave you an excuse you have not heard before, you might let him off the hook. Well I wanted to go to town and felt I had a good reason. I came here to ask your permission, but you were not in. I went to talk to the president, but he wasn't in either. So I decided to try the founder, and went out to Father Sorin's statue, and said, "Father, may I go to town?" There was no answer and so I took silence for consent.'

"The prefect admitted that he had never heard that one before...and added, 'And I'd better never hear it again!' "

– Professor Edward Fischer

"After one day here, most new freshmen have already been indoctrinated to touch the tiny toe of the three-foot founder's statue in the front hallway every time they pass. That's one way to verify that he hasn't been hijacked. In the 1950s it disappeared and for years afterward, university officials received periodic ransom notes with pictures of Father Sorin resting in front of various world wonders like the Eiffel Tower or the Great Wall.

"It is a committed thief who pays extra shipping charges for lugging a miniature priest around the globe in his suitcase. The TSA might prevent Father Sorin from skipping through airports so easily these days, but now he is safely anchored into our floor with a core of concrete and rebar that only an earthquake could topple."

– Fr. Jim King, C.S.C.,
Former Rector of Sorin Hall

Words of advice for parents from a hall rector who stands *in loco parentis*:

"Feed them with love, commitment, faith, generosity and humility. Teach them that they are among the most fortunate people on the earth and have an obligation to spend their lives giving more back. Take them to Disneyland, but bring them to a soup kitchen or nursing home once in a while too so they take nothing for granted.

"Fund their high school excursions to Italy, but make them work summers to pay for their gas money and video games so they understand that they have to earn what they get. Have them do practice tests because there are just some hoops even a seventeen-year-old must jump through, but tell them to revel in reading great literature and take college courses that make their souls sing and open up new worlds they hadn't imagined.

"Do spoil them—some. It's impossible not to be a soft touch once in a while if you love someone, but be a parent, not their best buds. They actually respect people who say no to them once in a while even if they don't like it right away.

"Embrace your daughter if she comes home pregnant and love her even more, but challenge your sons and daughters to consider what they would like to tell their own children someday about their own sexual activities during college. You don't even have to be religious to understand that we lead by example in all things but most of all in child-rearing.

"We gradually lose control as they age and have to let go for them to grow, but we can keep asking questions that raise the bar and cause them to ponder more deeply their own choices. Often a student who has a well-developed moral framework, even if it's not the one of my denomination, has all they need to make the right choice and avoid a disaster in a dicey situation.

"Some of you will do just about everything right and still get a phone call because your son or daughter got something wrong. Bad things happen to good kids, even in our protective Catholic Eden. The awful, random tragedies are the ones no priest wants to stand in a pulpit trying to explain.

"But, most of the time, the apple doesn't fall that far. I don't know whether it's more nature or nurture, but both ways the fruit ripens mainly at home. Since most of them seem to come out pretty well at the end of Senior Week, I figure most of you are good jugglers, but there are the occasional ones who would rather scream into the phone at me than peer deeper inside their own walls to figure out why their kid's life is so fouled up."

– Fr. Jim King, C.S.C.,
Former Rector of Sorin Hall

"It was one of our priests, Fr. Patrick Peyton, C.S.C., who coined the phrase, 'The family that prays together stays together.' Not to put down prayer, but he didn't nail it at all; he should have said 'prays *and eats*' together."

– Fr. Jim King, C.S.C.

"If we are afraid to be different from the world, how can we make a difference in the world?"

– Fr. John Jenkins, C.S.C., in his 2005
inaugural speech as President

"Institutionally, Notre Dame leans more toward Aquinas' confidence in grace building upon nature than Augustine's preoccupation with sin.

We do witness plenty of sinfulness in our students but even more evidence that Aquinas was right about human beings' natural inclinations. Most of them turn out pretty well in the end and some a lot better.

"We are a protective cocoon here, but the troubles of our times suggest that we should be fashioning more, rather than fewer, havens where tomorrow's heroes can nourish their ideals.

"A couple of years ago, I received a letter from a college friend who is a physician. He is content with his career, marriage and children and considers himself blessed. Nevertheless he regretted that he did not have more time to donate to those who lack access to the world's best medicine. I realize that his thoughts attest quite accurately to what a Notre Dame education should be and still remains at its best—a constant itch scratching our consciences long after the Dome has disappeared in the rear view mirror, compelling our graduates to ponder how they can spend the time they have doing more for those who have less."

– Fr. Jim King, C.S.C.

"The women at Notre Dame have brought soul to campus, mind to classroom, and also young, life-giving beauty to our campus. You do not have to plant flowers on a campus, but once you have seen what joy they bring the human heart, you would sorely miss them. God bless the women of Notre Dame."

– *Fr. Nicholas Ayo, C.S.C.*

"The saying that 'hurt people hurt people' is balanced by 'loved people love people.' Notre Dame students have been and are much loved, and they respond with much love and idealism. Their behavior is not always good, but their heart, more often than not, is in the right place.... Notre Dame students astonish us veterans with their persistent creativity for good, their initiative at home and abroad for helping the needy, their invention and generosity in undertaking what is new and seemingly impossible. The Center for Social Concerns at Notre Dame is the hub for much of this kind of activity beyond the campus, and daily care of one another in residence halls gives rise to the belief that love is as common as grass. We take in good people at Notre Dame; we pray that we turn them out even better."

– *Nicholas Ayo, C.S.C.*

"My gratitude to you is my prayer that each one of you young men and women on your graduation day shine forth as a bright light—the light of Christ—to the world around you.

"Feeding the hungry—not only with food but also with the Word of God.

"Giving drink to the thirsty—not only for water, but for knowledge, peace, truth, justice and love.

"Clothing the naked—not only with clothes, but also with human dignity.

"Giving shelter to the homeless—not only a shelter made of bricks, but a heart that understands, that covers, that loves.

"Nursing the sick and the dying—not only of the body but of the mind and Spirit....

"But to do this we need to be pure of heart for only the poor can see and recognize Jesus in the distressing disguise and touch Him in the poorest of the poor."

– Mother Teresa in a letter to the Notre Dame graduating class of 1986

"Next week, during fall vacation, students will find themselves wishing they were back in Indiana, near the Golden Dome. Before them, they will have the world with all its problems that need to be solved. Perhaps they will not readily have the solutions, but they do have the resources to find them because of the history that founds all that they learn each day at this University.

"Think of the faith of Sorin, the determination of Rockne, the courage of the Gipper and the sense of justice inherent in Hesburgh. Every moment spent here at Notre Dame is another moment for these legends to build students today just as they have built this school."

– Mary Anne Lewis, in the
Observer, *12/31/2003*

WHAT'S SO GREAT ABOUT NOTRE DAME?

The Golden Dome

The band marching through campus, playing "The Victory March" late afternoon on a football Friday

Monk Malloy, the president, living in a single room in one of the oldest residence halls on campus

Coeducation

A morning run around the lakes in autumn

Knute Rockne
Bookstore Basketball
Tom Dooley
Touchdown Jesus
The Congregation of Holy Cross
Interhall football in full pads
"Screw Your Roommate" dances
Junior Parents Weekend
The chariot race at An Tostal
Christmas in April
Neckties at Dinner
The abolition of Saturday classes
Student shows at the Snite
A midnight walk across a hushed campus in
    January when big flakes of snow are falling,
    turning everything serenely white
The stay hall system
Single sex dorms
Parietals
In loco parentis
UNDERC, LOBUND and the Medieval Institute
The Center for Tropical Disease Research and
    Training
Rad Lab
John Houck's ethics class
Meeting your favorite teacher at Pay Caf Oak
Room to talk
The Keenan Review
Freshman mixers

A Long John and Mellow Yellow at food sales in
    the basement of Farley
Sister Jean
The Bun Run
The Dog Book
The Milk Riots of 1951
The Beer Riots of 1984
The season's first big snowball fight
The hall chapels and dorm Masses
SUFR, GLAND, the PSA and ROTC
Notre Dame Encounter retreat weekends
Kegs 'n' eggs
Quarter dogs
Notre Dame and Yale cited as the nation's top two
    programs for the study of philosophy of
    religion
Notre Dame 71, UCLA 70 (January 19, 1974)
Vetville
The bachelor dons
The Prefect of Discipline
Going to class
Getting out of class
Basketball at the Rock
Basketball games at the old Fieldhouse
"Badin Bog Ball"
Burning calories while watching TV at Rolfs
SMC chicks
The squirrels

Kellogg, Kroc, Cushwa, Keough and the Institute
    for Latino Studies
Regis, Phil and Condoleezza
The Folk Choir singing at Mass in Sacred Heart
    Basilica
The Glee Club caroling in the women's halls
    during finals
Marshmallow wars at halftime
Architecture grads "styling" their mortarboards
    at commencement
The Center for Social Concerns
Eighty percent of all students doing volunteer
    service
The Collegiate Jazz Festival, Blues Festival and
    Sophomore Literary Festival
Seventy percent of all undergrads lettering in
    at least one varsity high school sport, with
    38 percent having been team captain
The leprechaun
The shirt
Stonehenge
The sprinklers watering the sidewalks
The 1960 Conference on Pornography and
    Censorship
Seven Heisman Trophy winners and
    11 National Championships
Driving up Notre Dame Avenue when the dome
is shining and the trees are orange, red, and
brilliant gold

A catholic Catholicism

Lights out at 10

6 a.m. sign-in at chapel

Frankie's, Corby's, Rosie's, Nickie's, Simeri's, Louie's, Rocco's, Sweeney's, Bridget's, Coach's, Boat Club, and the 'Backer

Sneaking in after midnight

Black Mac

The naked swim at freshman P.E.

Tackle football in a foot of snow

Circus lunch

The graffiti dance

Notre Dame 68, Purdue 66 (April 1, 2001)

Rudy

King Kersten

Ronald Reagan as The Gipper

Martin Sheen as Josiah Bartlet

The abduction and travels of the Sorin statue

Julian Samora

Playing flag football under the lights on the fields by Stepan

Studying on the 10th floor of the library

Study breaks on the second floor

George Craig, Morris Pollard and Laszlo Barabasi

The South Shore to Chicago

250 Notre Dame clubs throughout the world

Tyrone Willingham

CILA, ACE and the Andrews Summer Service Projects

Al Sondej

Monogrammed waffles at the South Dining Hall

The Huddle

Angiers, London, Innsbruck, Rome, Tantur,
Australia...Notre Dame first among major
U.S. research universities in the percentage
of students studying abroad

The road to Saint Mary's

Father Griffin and Darby O'Gill

Joe Evans

Frasier Thompson

The Gipper column in the *Scholastic*

The Observer at lunch

Ara, Leahy, Lou and Muffet

Meeting the team buses at the Circle

The ducks

A funeral ceremony for an alligator, complete
with chants, hymns, and burial behind Sorin
Hall (and the subsequent sermonizing in
The Religious Bulletin against the sacrilege
of mocking Catholic rituals, which should not
be made fun of under any circumstances)

The Religious Bulletin

Clashmore Mike

The fencing team

The Bengal Bouts

Wind tunnels, atom smashers and low-energy
nuclear physics

Expert advice on the Dead Sea Scrolls

Notre Dame 1, Portland 0 (December 3, 1995)

John O'Hara, CSC

Moose Krause

The Irish Guard

The Fisher Regatta

Pep rallies in Stepan

Pep rallies in the Old Fieldhouse with its balcony
and beams, dirt floors and aging brick walls

Ranking in the top 20 both academically
(*U.S.News and World Report*) and athletically
(the NACDA Directors Cup standings)

"Molarity" by Michael Molinelli daily in
The Observer

Maid service

Laundry service

Roommates

The Basilica bells tolling the hours

Siegfried freshmen getting their horns

The NBC contract

Alan Page, Chris Zorich and Ruth Riley

Nobel Laureate Eric Wieschaus

Nobel Peace Prize Laureate Elie Wiesel

Dennis Jacobs, the 2003 U.S. Professor of
the Year

Late-night coffee and conversation at Reckers

"You can talk about God here and no one
snickers." – Norman Mailer

Watching *Knute Rockne All American* in
   Washington Hall
"(O)ne of America's most wired campuses"
The sitting U.S. President coming to campus to
   speak
Moratorium Day, 1969
Fifteen minutes to cease and desist
Notre Dame graduates getting accepted into med
   school at a rate twice the national average
The accounting department always in the top 10
The law school among the top four in teaching
   quality
Springtime on the south quad, lying on a blanket
   reading *One Hundred Years of Solitude* with
   music and Frisbees flying through the air
The 9/11 outdoor Mass
The look on the face of a freshman moving her
   stuff into Lyons
The look on the faces of her parents during
   commencement
The Grotto in springtime, when the western sky
   is rosy with sunlight at dusk
The Grotto in autumn, when the canopy trees are
   radiant and the leaves are underfoot
The Grotto in winter, when the candles glow and
   snow blankets the night
The seniors singing "Notre Dame, Our Mother"
   at the end of the final home game

Emil T. Hoffman
Frank O'Malley
Theodore M. Hesburgh, CSC

– *From* Notre Dame Magazine

"Life under the Dome usually has the seriousness of purpose that it deserves. Yet, any good community can laugh at its foibles and appreciate the occasional creative antic. Students in particular are always ready to maximize the fun that common life allows for. It can be anything from the phantom phone call, to the dunk in the lake, to the generous use of shaving cream or hot sauce. Students pull pranks on each other, their rectors, and on their teachers (if they are really brave). Still, not all the laughs are at someone's expense. Sometimes just youthful exuberance is enough to carry the day. And then there are all the organized (some loosely) shows, satires and entertainments that offer commentary on campus life, on youth culture, or the media, and on the political scene. Some among us have an innate gift for imitation and there is always plenty of material for the astute observer."

– *Fr. Edward A. Malloy, C.S.C., President Emeritus*

"When people ask about Notre Dame's loyalty, about the mystique of Notre Dame, I tell them it is really made up of many separate elements, but I think no part of it is more critical than the residential tradition of the institution. It's funny that often the students who complain the most about the rules when they are here, later want their kids to come here. In fact, I can remember that the parents of the students who are here now got in the same trouble that their kids get in, but that is a story for another day."

– Rev. Edward "Monk" Malloy, C.S.C.

"And it [the feeling of Notre Dame] pervades the campus. It hangs like the clouds, penetrates like a breeze. This special closeness, holiness, concern is found in the students, in the faculty, in the very buildings, structure and history of Notre Dame.... the specialness is transportable, it never leaves Notre Dame. It is still encased here, still vibrant, moving, tangible, prodding its students while enrapturing them..."

– Louise Giunti ... Scholastic *1983*

"I loved my time at ND and have been active at the Law School since graduation in 1968. Every good thing that's happened to me can be traced to Notre Dame. The lessons I learned from ND shaped my life and the friends I made are life-long. My work for ND is my way of saying thank you. I tell people that my body left ND in 1968 but my heart is still there."

– Thomas R. Curtin '68

"I said a lot of rosaries."

– A student's response to his professor asking,
"How did you ever get into Notre Dame?"

Speaking at his final commencement as President [2005], Fr. Monk Malloy gave graduates three pieces of advice:
"Cherish your friends.
Remain open to change and surprise.
Make room for God in your life's routine."

"The essential beauty of Notre Dame, I think, is its people and the variegated dimensions of their lives, and the various rituals that bring us together—in play and prayer and service."

– *Kerry Temple*

"Every year, after return to campus from spring break and about the time of the feast day of St. Joseph in March, the largest basketball tournament in the world commences at the University of Notre Dame. More than 500 teams are formed. Students play alongside faculty and staff members. The president of the University joins a team and the football coach as well. Varsity athletes play with rank amateurs. Women and men play on the same team. Some teams have not a prayer, but they play to join the party. Some clown on the court, and others play with razzle-dazzle. Height and weight count, but fast and sharp count even more in this streetwise basketball on asphalt courts, whatever the weather: rain or snow. Only one varsity athlete per team is allowed, but the occasional unknown perimeter shooter makes you wonder if he or she should not be a walk-on for the varsity. They name themselves, and some team names are hilarious and others so 'colorful' they are censored. Elimination competition halves the number of teams quickly. At the end, a final four emerge, and then there are only two. The winning team is likely not the biggest or the most talented, but the one with the indomitable heart, artful strategy and deadly shooting. Teamwork will win the day. The competition is democratic. The whole campus is involved. At times there are rivalries along the lines of race or residence. The courtside commentary can be as cruel as the pavement is hard, but in the end, the Notre Dame campus has pulled together, either as player or fan....Were Joseph of Nazareth here, I think he would have played himself and taught Jesus how to play, and Mary, too. It's a family thing. We all belong, and all the pieces of our days belong to God's providential plan for our own welfare."

– Fr. Nicholas Ayo, C.S.C.,
Professor Emeritus, General Program

"Junior Parents Weekend at Notre Dame has become a heart-touching visit of mothers and fathers, who are hosted by their children. What is said and done on this weekend leaves a memory treasured by everyone involved on campus.

Typically the weather in late February presents dark, cold winter.

"Some years these parents show their love in just fighting the elements and arriving in South Bend at all. One hears stories of parents stranded in the Chicago airport who rented cars and drove together to Notre Dame despite the snowstorm. The heartfelt invitation and the response, not withstanding an inconvenient journey, reveal how often the medium is the message. Parents love their children, and on this weekend, their children tell them of their love in hospitality given and perhaps also in words spoken.

"I have always thought the junior year the best of the four years of college. In the first year of studies (called freshman year before coeducation), the students are not yet altogether here. Part of each of them is homesick. Sophomores have read all of Plato but do not know they do not know. In their salad days, they are crisp but quite green. Seniors are already part gone, for their heart has already begun to imagine the future and to prepare to say goodbye. But the juniors are here body and soul, and they are in the main mature in mind and in heart....I have known and taught junior-class students who are so alive with the yearning to know, so capable of generous heart combined with ample knowledge.

They remain grateful and thoughtful, ready in every way to host on campus the mother and father who gave them life, who taught them to tie their shoes, and who gave them human language and family love as the wealth of kings and queens—and paid their tuition and more at Notre Dame. Junior Parents Weekend is simply wonderful."

– Fr. Nicholas Ayo, C.S.C.

"I think the university is delighted that St. Patrick's Day usually falls during spring break. The troubles of the few who cannot contain themselves do not trouble the campus. Any yet, trouble is a teaching moment. I know that alums come back to the university to see their rectors more than their teachers. They came back to see 'Black Mac' (Father Charles McCarragher, who ran a tight ship in the dorm and patrolled the bars at night). They came back to see the 'Sneakin' Deacon' (Fr. Paul Fryberger, who legend claims ran down the dorm corridor to quiet a party with one shoe and one sneaker so that he seemed to be walking along slowly). Alums come back with gratitude for those men and women who lived with them in their residence halls and dealt with their first mistakes in a way that led them to grow up....The Notre Dame campus is a great place for a party on St. Patrick's Day and a great place to learn, with some help, how to be responsible for one's choices and indeed the outcome of one's whole life. Bishop St. Patrick would understand and approve."

– Fr. Nicholas Ayo, C.S.C.

"Senior Week fills the days between the end of final exams and the following Graduation Week-end. This campus has been home to the graduating seniors. For a long time, their residence halls have been home. These roommates and these friends—from classes, hall life, clubs, choirs, sports and what have you—have become lifetime friends who shared for some years this home together. Good-byes are painful even when time is provided for the last days to linger in the heart. The last visits to the Basilica and to the Grotto give many students memories for a lifetime.... Awards are given out on the Saturday before graduation...With tears in my eyes I look for the ones I know, and I think if the future depends on such wonderful men and women as these, the future is in good hands. From them will come governors and judges, teachers and newspaper editors, museum directors and doctors. Just about any vocation is open to them. Their problem will be an embarrassment of riches. So many choices, just one precious life to live."

– *Fr. Nicholas Ayo, C.S.C.*

"John Broderick, a professor at the Law School and known as the Chief, phoned me one day and asked me to say a few words at his law class rally [which he conducted in his class on the Wednesday before every home football game]. I can't recall how much time I spent putting together an outline of what I was going to say because I really wanted to do a good job for Chief Broderick and his class. I came to his class totally prepared. I met the Chief, a bandy rooster type of individual, before the class began. He told me where to sit, make myself comfortable, and then he disappeared. The law students filed in and took their seats. Suddenly the music of the 'Notre Dame Victory March' resonated wall to wall over the speaker system as Chief Broderick stormed into the classroom waving an Irish shillelagh. He was wearing a kelly green hat, an ancient oversized green plaid sport coat that was adorned with a multitude of assorted Irish football pins and a couple of bumper stickers. The applause, cheering and shouting from the students was enough to shatter eardrums. The Chief quieted them down, introduced me and told his class I had a few words to say and to listen carefully. It led to more applause, cheering, shouts, and so forth, and it didn't stop. I was unable to say a word. Then the Chief raised his hand, quieted the class, and said, 'Thank you, Sergeant McCarthy, you may sit down.' I was stunned. I never said a word. Then Chief introduced two football players he had invited. Each stood up to say a few words and the same thing happened. They weren't able to say a word. The Chief sat them down and wielding his shillelagh he immediately led the class in a rousing Notre Dame cheer. After that, the speaker system again blasted out that rousing rendition of the 'Victory March.' Then it suddenly became quiet. Next was the grand finale of playing the school anthem, 'Notre Dame Our Mother,' as the law class sang along with it, linked arm-in-arm. The rally was over. Lasting about fifteen minutes, it went bang, bang, bang. What a great routine by the Chief. No one was able to say anything except the Chief; that is how he always conducted his rally. Looking back, it was the most spirited Notre Dame rally I ever attended."

– *Sergeant Tim McCarthy*

"David Ruffer has not forgotten where he comes from. If he did, he wouldn't be able to find his room.

"The nation's most accurate walk-on kicker still lives in Siegfried Hall on Notre Dame's campus, a spot from which the journey to Notre Dame Stadium is more winding than one might think.

"When he can, Ruffer still attends interhall football games, where his implausible story began. He was a high school golfer. He played soccer for one year. He never played football. After transferring to Notre Dame in 2008, he kicked for Siegfried and was plucked for a tryout with the Irish.

"Now, no one in Notre Dame history has made more consecutive field goals than Ruffer. With 11 in a row this year alone, he's at 16 and counting himself astounded. All three members of the kicking operation—including snapper Bill Flavin and holder Ryan Kavanagh—are walk-ons. Asked to describe his expectations of a walk-on kicker, Irish coach Brian Kelly went with 'very low.' 'I don't tell him a knock-knock joke on the way out there,' Kavanagh said. 'I try to make sure he's focused on the right things and not stressing about everything. I don't say, 'Hey, if you make this, you're the all-time leading kicker in Notre Dame history, no pressure.'"

– Chicago Tribune *sportswriter Brian Hamilton*

"You're not coming in here dressed like *that*!"
– Sr. Jean Lenz, O.F.M.

Now the whole story leading up to this quote:

"Spring is a noisy time on campus, bursting with spontaneous eruptions of all sorts.... It was in the spirit of such revelry that I received a call from the not-yet ordained rector in Grace Hall, Bob Wiseman, warning me that a group of young men were running toward Farley Hall 'full of springtime.' It was near midnight. I had other things on my mind as I corrected theology papers. In the midst of a certain calmness on the floors overhead with dimmed night-lights filling the hallways, I suddenly heard the disturbing, heavily-throated chant, 'Farley, Farley, Farley.' I swished around the corner of my doorway, ran down three steps, and stood guard at the south entrance breathing the words, 'They're not getting in here tonight.' With the grace of office and rector boldness, I pushed the door open as someone inserted an electronic Detex passcard from the outside, saying with such triumph to the troops behind him, 'It works!' And that's when the drama peaked.

"I swung the door open toward the crowd that was an arm's length away, only to discover some hundred young men ready to charge the hall in their birthday suits. I remember cupping my hands around my mouth and shouting at the top of my lungs, 'You're not coming in here dressed like *that*!' Then I heard a great holler, a strong voice rise above the rest, declaring the state of affairs, 'Oh no, it's Sister Jean,' and a great scrambling retreat was underway. Some made a fast getaway and dove into the nearest bushes next to Farley's doorway, others ran for the bushes that lined the north wall of Breen-Phillips Hall. Some jumped behind bicycles nearby and peeked through the spokes of wheels, while others simply stood frozen on the spot, a bit in shock, with twisted backs facing me.

"I stood in the doorway until I heard a leading cry of brotherhood from the bushes that injected bravery into the troops as they began to move back toward Farley. This time they came toward me stumbling backward. Again in this fleshy atmosphere of strong male backsides, I said, 'I told you, you're not getting in here like that.' There was another retreat and a halfhearted third attempt to enter, upon which I shouted, 'I am not moving from this spot until you fellows move on.' Then came the final rallying cry, 'Let's get Lyons Hall.' I dashed to the phone and called the Lyons rector who would have time to gather her personnel and bolt all entrances against these brave marauders of springtime. Her answer was one grand sigh.

"When I caught my breath and realized that Farley's security guard, Hazel, had been beside me all the time, I turned to her and said, 'Am I dreaming or did this really just happen?' Then I heard the clapping of Farley residents from the shadows of the hallway behind me and I knew I was awake."

– Sr. Jean Lenz, O.F.M.

"Snow calls forth all kinds of sculpturing instincts and creativity. Some of the best art pieces occurred during the great snowfall of 1978, when forty inches fell from January 25-27. In all, 130 inches of snow were recorded that winter, eighty-six of which fell in January, breaking all South Bend records. The University was officially closed for five days....For winter daredevils, a 'snow-chute' was created by packing mounds of snow onto the front steps of the Main Building. The aim of the game was to see who could get closest to the Sacred Heart statue, riding on a dining-room tray."

– Sr. Jean Lenz, O.F.M.

"Farley's laundry room was a perfect setting for a sitcom. Until undergraduate women were admitted to the University, there was only St. Michael's general campus laundry, designed primarily to handle clothing for the male population. Women's residence halls added new laundry facilities to campus, which quickly caught the attention of the men who lived in the vicinity.

"Grace and Flanner Halls were each one thousand residents strong, and many of these students found endless ways to sneak into Farley to use one of seven washers and dryers....On one of my laundry rounds, I discovered one lad who was not only new to the facility, but also new to the machinery. I stopped him from adding another dose of Tide detergent onto a load of clothes he had stuffed into a dryer.

"A Grace Hall senior confessed one day that he actually sneaked into Farley and got away with washing his 'good shirts' on more than one occasion. Initially the joke was on him, he insisted, since it took him weeks to realize that he was supposed to add soap to each load. He thought once you inserted the necessary coins, soap was automatically added."

– *Sr. Jean Lenz, O.F.M.*

"When Jason Steidl moved into Room 306 Carroll Hall, he had no idea he was living in a room that once sheltered a future Catholic saint. 'I feel like I won the lottery,' said Steidl, a graduate student in theology and assistant rector of Carroll Hall, a men's residence hall on the southwestern edge of St. Mary's Lake at the University of Notre Dame.

"Blessed Brother André Bessette, a French Canadian brother who was known as the 'Miracle Man of Montreal' for the miraculous cures attributed to him, will be canonized Sunday at a Mass in Rome. A friend to the poor and sick, Bessette always insisted that any such cures were attributable to the prayers of St. Joseph. The religious brother, who died in 1937 at age 91, is the first member of the Congregation of Holy Cross—Notre Dame's founding religious community—to be named a saint.

"Bessette visited South Bend and Notre Dame in July 1920 during a congregation General Chapter gathering. He and the other Canadian brothers were lodged in Dujarie Institute, which was the seminary for Holy Cross brothers. (It later was renamed Carroll Hall and turned into a residence hall for male undergraduates.)

" 'Frère André had the room, the third from the north end, on the west side of the house. It is now (Room) 306,' Brother Kilian Beirne wrote in a 1966 book, *From Sea to Shining Sea*, a history of the Holy Cross brothers."

– Margaret Fosmoe in the South Bend Tribune

"Father Marr addressed us one night in the chapel: 'I would like to remind you gentlemen that Walsh Hall is dedicated to the Blessed Virgin Mary, and she is the only one welcome here. If I see a lady above the first floor, I shall extend her the courtesy of asking her whether she is the Blessed Virgin, and if she says she is not, I shall ask her to leave.' "

– Jerome Ledvina '38

"The best college talk is high-minded, in the midnight hours, searching, groping for goals and God."

– Professor Tom Stritch

"The notion of teamwork, of cooperation, of making up for each other's deficiencies applies to institutions of all kinds, including universities."

– *Fr. Edward A. Malloy, C.S.C.*

"For those nurtured on its campus and proud of its traditions and spirit, Notre Dame evokes a sense of family...there is a bond that links the generations and makes them comfortable with the symbols, sites and songs of the place."

– *Fr. Edward A. Malloy C.S.C.*

FATHER HESBURGH'S TEN COMMANDMENTS FOR STUDENT LEADERS

1. Look upon all of it as a learning experience.
2. Mistakes are inevitable. You have to learn to live with them and so did I.
3. Don't get caught up with global issues, such as remaking the whole University and outgunning the Trustees. Politics is the art of the possible, so pick out some realistic goals and really go for them.

4. Try to strike up a friendship with the administration. They aren't really bad guys and you might have something to learn from them. Also, they are not automatic adversaries. Believe it or not, they like you and want to be helpful as you mature into real leaders.

5. The common good is terribly important. It means the common good for students, faculty and the whole University community. You are part of it, so work for it.

6. Be honest, especially with yourselves. Integrity is probably the best quality of a leader.

7. Be open-minded. No other attitude makes learning possible. As Winston Churchill noted, "All complicated problems have simple answers. However, they are all wrong."

8. Be fair even with grown-ups. Fairness will win them more than anything else.

9. Don't be cynical. A cynic accomplishes nothing. All of us have to be shocked by the injustices we face in life. Cynicism will never conquer them and attain justice.

10. This will probably sound silly, but my bottom line is laughter and love. It is important to be able to laugh at ourselves which means not to take ourselves too seriously, whether we are President or freshman. Somehow laughter gets us through the most difficult of

solutions, but love is important, too, because in a very real sense, we can't work together unless we respect and love each other, young and old.

"The mystique of Notre Dame, that seemingly incomprehensible measure of loyalty and devotion to the University that characterizes so many of our graduates and friends, is best explained through the on-campus living experience of the students....The residence halls are places where values are clarified, friendships are formed, and faith is tested and professed. There is nothing to replace simply being here through the cycles of the seasons and the years."

– Fr. Edward A. Malloy, C.S.C.,
President Emeritus

"Notre Dame is also a community. It must therefore attend with care and compassion to the well being of all its members...the creation of community at Notre Dame is a family-like thing, the wish that there be no strangers here.

"Yet, like all families, we also suffer our misunderstandings and disputes. At times, we neglect the needful in our midst, we stereotype minorities, and we treat with disdain those flauntingly different. Regretfully, we allow gender or race or status and rank to fracture our commonality and drive us apart. In recognition of this inconsistency and harm, we ever need to acknowledge our failure and move to reform our common life.

"Notre Dame is and must be a community. For only thus can it be true to its call."

– Fr. Edward A. Malloy, C.S.C.

(Let it be noted that under Father Malloy's administration, great strides were made in expanding diversity in the student body, faculty and administration of Notre Dame, an improvement that continues under his successor, Fr. John I. Jenkins, C.S.C.)

"College students, by nature, are inclined to think they can change the world, but Notre Dame students are more inclined than most actually to try."

– Author Kevin Coyne

"I encourage my students to really interrogate their relationship with the media-saturated world that surrounds them," he says. "When you introduce different ways of looking critically at what seems so familiar, a kind of pedagogical spontaneous combustion can occur—and it's those golden moments that are the most rewarding. I have no interest at all in simply downloading information."

– *Professor Jim Collins, Sheedy Award winner, 2010*

"You can go to college anywhere and get a good education, but Notre Dame will change your life."

– *Kerry Temple*

"What I feel fairly certain of is if Notre Dame is to remain a vital center of Catholic learning throughout the third millennium, we must create an undergraduate environment that encourages and rewards original thinking, experimentation, conversation, the unfettered engagement of great texts and ideas, open-ended exploration, and unabashed dreaming.

– *Hugh R. Page, Jr., Dean of Freshman Year of Studies, Notre Dame*

"Notre Dame winters seem to defy the laws of physics. In whatever direction you head across campus, you walk against the wind."

– Kerry Temple, '74

"Though gender relations on campus would appear to still be in need of improvement, the young women of Notre Dame have improved this campus immeasurably. For my money, women are the best thing that happened to Notre Dame since it was named after one.

– Matthew Storin

"The sounds of music and laughter emanate from the cozy confines where roommates study, tease and taunt, sometimes console in hushed tones. Real living takes place here, where bunks and lofts, rectors and friends and decks and all manner of electronic devices crowd into these flourishing cells of human habitation. Indeed, this just might be the very place where the real education takes place, where the ideas, dreams and theories get plumbed and tested to see if they mesh or clash with the inescapable, in-your-face reality of daily life in earnest. Where everything is personal. Where you can never really get away."

– Kerry Temple

"It is hard to believe that forty years ago, I began my undergraduate studies at Notre Dame. And I have come full circle, as my office now is right next to the classroom where I took English Literature as a freshman....I remember the professor looking directly at me and asking what it meant when Huck Finn was floating down the river and clouds were forming overhead. I quickly froze and then stammered, 'It meant it was going to rain.' When the classmates' laughter ended, the professor kindly responded that 'perhaps the clouds signified the coming storms in his life.' Now I still can't say I totally agree with him; but I honestly believe I haven't read a book in the same way since! Notre Dame opened up the world to me by challenging me to look at things differently."

– Daniel Saracino, former
Assistant Provost, Admissions

"Nothing renders a man so unfit for study as excessive exercise."

– Fr. John Cavanaugh, C.S.C., in 1887

On the lighter side, Notre Dame students are able to poke fun at themselves, as is evident in recent graduate Bob Kessler's book, *Things Notre Dame Students Like*:

"#29: Telling people when they have an organic chemistry exam

"Of all the students and all of the majors at Notre Dame, the most notoriously neurotic are Pre-Meds, and throughout their four years preparing for medical school, the most infamous class they must take is Organic Chemistry (commonly referred to as Orgo).

"While Pre-Med students famously bitch and moan about most of their coursework, their whining hits a remarkable high during their sophomore year when they take Orgo. For an entire year, these students incessantly complain about how difficult the class is and how much studying they have to do for it. By way of their complaints, these students make it known to the entire Notre Dame community how unrelenting the class is and when the class faces exams.

"The level of whining wouldn't be much of a problem for the rest of the student body if it weren't for the Orgo students' insistence on telling everybody when they have an upcoming test. An Orgo student would probably never know if their Political Science roommate had an upcoming exam, but this isn't a two-way street. The days and even weeks before an Orgo test are marred by reminders that the test is coming. Orgo students will continuously refuse to go out, or even eat meals with other students, and will make sure to use the upcoming Orgo test as their excuse.

"Orgo students mark their territory in the library: some sleep in study rooms, while others even make the crucial error of studying before football games in an attempt to be overly prepared. The tension in the dorms on the night before an Orgo text is higher than any other night. While Pre-Meds are tweaked out on Red Bull and RockStar, drawing diagrams on whiteboards and spreading papers and textbooks around study rooms, their roommates and friends look for ways to avoid the madness for fear of causing bodily harm to themselves and others.

"Despite the fact that Pre-Meds spend an unnecessary amount of time preparing for Orgo exams, and make sure to let everybody know it, they perform remarkably poorly on these exams. In fact these students brag about how poorly they do on Orgo tests just to prove to their peers how difficult the class is (they'll never mention the ridiculous test curve just in case they happen to actually fail the next one). A good percentage of these students take these poor test scores as a sign and end up switching to a more reasonable major where students aren't as psychotic, because as difficult as Pre-Med majors claim that Organic Chemistry is, one year later they will be making similarly apocalyptic claims as they study for the MCATS—a test that makes all students go crazy, even if they don't take it."

Also from Bob Kessler's book is this entertaining tidbit:

Days Notre Dame Students Like

1. USC game [only in odd years]
2. Day/night before the USC game [only in odd years]
3. First Friday of the fall semester [or whenever each dorm throws Dis-Orientation]
4. First home game
5. Saint Patrick's Day
6. Michigan game [an even-year replacement for #1]
7. Room picks [varies depending on dorm]

8. Blue-Gold game [mainly due to PigTostal]
9. First day of spring [completely random day when girls wear skirts and people play games on the quad]
10. First big snowfall of the winter
11. The day the annual ND-SMC Viewpoint war reaches its zenith
12. First day of winter study days [due to Christmas parties]
13. Last night dorms are open in the spring
14. First bookstore basketball games
15. Day beer garden re-opens at Corby's

Another favorite excerpt from Kessler's book certainly would be:

"#65 Riding bikes in adverse conditions
"One of the great things about Notre Dame's campus is that the residential and academic buildings are all relatively close together. Students can easily walk between the most distant buildings of importance (so, not including Carroll) without exerting an inordinate amount of time or effort. This pedestrian campus is promoted by an abundance of sidewalks and a lack of cars on campus.

"Despite the convenient layout of campus, many students still feel the need to pretend they are going to a large state school by riding their bikes between buildings. Because of the short distances, these students will undoubtedly spend more time locking their bikes than they will actually riding them (because locking bikes is necessary to prevent them from being stolen—or even worse, finding them hanging in a tree somewhere).

"While this biking may be simply a leisure activity in the warm months, Notre Dame Students inexplicably continue to ride their bikes in the inclement weather that lasts from October until May. Whether through snow, sleet, ice, hail, wind, or rain, the biking contingent of Notre Dame Students is relentless. These students will put plastic bags on the seats of their bikes to ensure dryness, and then they will hit the ice-covered sidewalks in their perilous quest from their dorm to DeBartolo Hall to the dining hall and back. Never worrying about the inevitable loss of traction, these students will slide across the sidewalk, crash into pedestrians, and get even wetter than their more sensible walking counterparts.

"Ultimately, most students will realize that bicycles simply were not built to be ridden around in the adverse conditions of a South Bend winter. However, these students will choose not to leave their bike in one place throughout the winter, but will walk their bike across the slick and icy sidewalks so that it will still be with them when the day comes that conditions are more desirable for biking."

One more enjoyable Kessler list that many will relate to is the following:

Things Notre Dame Alumni Like

1. Complaining about the football team, regardless of what happens on the field
2. Threatening to halt donations
3. Hiring ND students
4. Reminiscing about the bars at five corners
5. Complaining about Tom Hammond and Pat Hayden (especially in HD)
6. Getting indignant about losing Catholic identity
7. Using the word "draconian" to describe University policies
8. Dorm Mass after football games
9. The Sorin Society and other donation-based organizations
10. Talking about how they couldn't get into ND if they applied today
11. Ara Parseghian
12. Knowing the lyrics to now-obscure school songs
13. Buying property in South Bend

14. Anonymously sponsoring parties in their old dorm room or house
15. Complaining about the football schedule
16. Vanity license plates
17. Being quiet during football games while complaining about a lack of noise in the stadium
18. Having a full bar at their family tailgate
19. Pep rallies (both talking about how awesome they used to be in the old Fieldhouse and actively contributing to the modern incarnation being significantly less awesome)
20. Monogram sweater-vests
21. Hoping their local city hosts an off-site game, and then complaining about the existence of the off-site games
22. Playing catch with their children on South Quad
23. Lamenting the loss of the University Club
24. Being randomly generous to current students
25. Having their kids attend the University of Notre Dame

And of course, the principal thing that Notre Dame students like is:

"#100: Notre Dame

"Notre Dame Students like a lot of things. They like things that are related to their religion and how they are always using Catholicism to guide their actions (even if just for the sake of appearing to be more Catholic than they really are). They like things that pertain to their academic plight and how they firmly believe that Notre Dame is one of the most prestigious schools in the world (and how each of them is personally the smartest and most clever person one could ever meet). They like things that have to do with their dorms and the crazy things that happen when a random collection of individuals is brought together to create a long-lasting community. Notre Dame Students like things that are related to drinking and how, no matter how hard they work, they still know how to party hard. And they like football. Notre Dame Students like their football and the tradition-filled Saturdays that made the school what it is today. Most of all, and this might seem a bit obvious, but they like what happens when all of these things come together: they like Notre Dame.

"Notre Dame Students like the feeling they get when they walk to class across South Quad on a sunny day, when the shining Golden Dome catches their eye. They like the feeling they get when they're driving back to campus after a break and see that billboard for The Bookstore on I-80 coming from Chicago, and know they are almost there. They like the feeling they get when they're recognized as a Notre Dame student because they're wearing a monogrammed hat in a bar far from campus. They love how it feels when they're standing in a crowd of their peers, trying to enter Notre Dame Stadium before kickoff and yelling at the top of their lungs:

"Goooooooooooooo IRISH,

Beeeeeeeeeeeeat TROJANS!!

"Notre Dame Students like all of these things and more, but most of all they like knowing that, of all the colleges they could have chosen at which to spend their four years, they came to a place with a tradition of excellence where the past meets the present, and the future isn't too far ahead. They love the fact that they wound up at a place that truly is unique, where every day presents an opportunity for them to be a part of something special, and they love the fact that of all the students that still dream of going there, they were chosen by the University to make Notre Dame their home."

– *Bob Kessler*

Student Room – circa 1893

SPIRIT AND SPIRITUALITY

"Reverence for God is the main reason for Notre Dame's existence."

– Edward Fischer '37

"Dying is no big deal. The least of us will manage that. Living is the trick."

– Red Smith '27

"What do I hope for or ask of the class of '73? Why only this: that using your private sources of grace, you establish absolutes of decency, gentleness, and service; and then that you live as witnesses of the truths you could die for."

– Fr. Robert Griffin, C.S.C.

"I don't know to this day why I chose Notre Dame. I just thought I'd like to go there and that was all right with my father. I'm delighted Notre Dame accepted me. I love the place."

– Edwin O'Connor '39, author of
The Edge of Sadness *and* The Last Hurrah

"In a hundred years, Notre Dame will still be Notre Dame. Some things will change, others will stay the same. Old faces will give way and new faces will take their place. Buildings will be built with bricks different from the ancient yellow bricks of Sorin's time. The place will survive."

– Fr. Robert Griffin, C.S.C.

"How is God better glorified than by intelligent and devoted service to others in the line of our chosen life's work. Neither God nor mankind is well served by mediocrity."

– Rev. Theodore Hesburgh, C.S.C.

"If we, young and old, can agree on those basic values that make human life worth living, then perhaps we can pool our efforts to redeem the time. It still won't be easy, but it can be done."

– Rev. Theodore M. Hesburgh, C.S.C.

"…(A) university such as Notre Dame is bricks and books, classrooms and laboratories. But it is, above all, people. Some come here for four years, perhaps to return only in spirit, while others' very lives revolve around this place. I like to think that Notre Dame makes its mark on all who come here, and not a few make their mark on Notre Dame."

– Rev. Theodore M. Hesburgh, C.S.C.

"Where fervor and devotion reign, a sacrifice is a joy rather than an affliction."

– Fr. Edward Sorin, C.S.C.

"Indeed, *if* physical trials and hardships had overcome the Fathers of Notre Dame, the little cabin on your campus would represent the limit of their missionary efforts in the great Midwest.

"*If* the struggle against poverty had broken the spirits of your parents and grandparents, there would never have been the resources to send you here to obtain the benefits of Catholic culture.

"*If* seemingly overwhelming odds meant surrender, there never would have been the glorious tradition of Notre Dame's athletic prowess, for indeed it is the will to win regardless of the odds that stirred this nation under the symbol of 'the fighting Irish.'

"*If* misfortune crushed Notre Dame, then the great fire of 1879, which wiped out every University building except the chapel and the theater would have written 'Finis' to Notre Dame. But in the two remaining buildings—the chapel and the stage of life upon which generations should perpetuate Catholic teaching—there was a symbolic and prophetic meaning for the Fathers of Notre Dame.

"*If* the Fathers of the noble Congregation of Holy Cross had fastened their gaze upon earth alone and placed their prize upon the praise of men, there never would have been the grotto by the lake where stalwart generations of Notre Dame men have knelt reverently in deep devotion and prayer to God."

– Joseph P. Kennedy, Commencement Speech, 1941

"Notre Dame is a place, a sequence in time, an immediate living fact all wrapped round with people."

– Professor Richard Sullivan

"Good teaching is a sort of sacramental action, a communication of spirit."

– Fr. John W. Cavanaugh, C.S.C.

"In the eyes of God, merit is not always gauged by success or by the development of enterprise."

– Fr. Edward Sorin, C.S.C.

"If the vision of this institution is special and unique, it is because we cherish faith and values. Absent or present both of them, education and life are different."

– Fr. Theodore Hesburgh, C.S.C.

"As members of the Notre Dame family scattered throughout the world, we cannot remain impassive in the face of the challenge modern day society presents to us. Our duty lies in becoming knights of human dignity, who with our shields of 'gold and blue' defend the humble of the world."

– Jose Napoleon Duarte, former President of El Salvador, Commencement, 1985

"For those proud of its traditions and spirit, Notre Dame evokes a sense of family…there is a bond that links the generations and makes them comfortable with the symbols and songs of the place."

– Edward A. "Monk" Malloy, C.S.C.

"The foundational love for thousands of families, religious vows, and forms of self-giving more difficult to categorize, has been received or discovered during strolls around the lakes."

– Michael Garvey, Assistant Director/
Public Information/Communication, Notre Dame

"I want you to know that last September, I pulled for Stanford, but I prayed for Notre Dame...

"Here at Notre Dame you have been especially privileged to be in a place where the commitment to reason and the will to know exist side by side with faith and belief. The simultaneous right to question and the ability to accept on the basis of faith is at the core of this place. It is not always easy for the educated person to find the integration of faith and reason, particularly in a world that often denies that which cannot be proven, that which cannot be seen."

– Condoleezza Rice, ND Alumna;
Provost, Stanford University;
U.S. Secretary of State

"This is the kind of place you dream of, but never think you will go there. That is exactly how I felt. You had to pinch yourself for four years almost that you were really here. I want my children to go to Notre Dame. You can't give them a better gift than Notre Dame. I mean I still, every time I talk about it, I get emotional and choked up about it because it was one of the best things my parents ever gave me."

– Alumna Veronica Guzman/Gutierrez

"Remember, gentlemen, at Notre Dame you are a student-athlete." Father Hesburgh to incoming freshmen basketball stars, 1967. Recalls Austin Carr, "I came away from that meeting feeling that these men [Frs. Hesburgh and Joyce] cared about me outside of basketball and that they would be like parents away from home."

(Cited in 100 Years of Notre Dame Basketball, *"Foreword" by Austin Carr 2004, University of Notre Dame Sports Information)*

"That's one characteristic of Notre Dame that everybody should get to experience at one point —come up here and see the atmosphere and see how close-knit the whole Notre Dame family is."

– Former basketball star Torrian Jones

"No one person can have the answers; we are all finding our way together, even when we find ourselves at odds over the correct paths to take."

– David Burrell, C.S.C.

"A teacher can teach well or badly in any school, and a plumber need not fret much about the source of his or her paycheck. But decent PR [public relations] people (and there are more of them than you might imagine) need to be a bit more self-conscious. I would argue that Notre Dame is one of those exceptional institutions in which it is possible simultaneously to practice public relations and to maintain one's integrity."

– Michael Garvey

"I think all of us who work here are obligated to offer our students an unabashedly parental love, welcoming them into a community of religious belief, intellectual inquiry, and devotion to the weak. It is a family in which we elders, who are here longer than four years, are, for a time and whether they like it or not, their parents. The most important thing parents teach their children is what to love, and the only way to teach children what to love is by loving what is worthy of one's love."

– Michael Garvey

"As Pope Paul VI noted, 'The [Virgin Mary] is held up as an example to the faithful for the way in which in her own life she fully and responsibly accepted the will of God, because she heard the word of God and acted on it, and because charity and a spirit of service were the driving force of her actions. She is worthy of imitation because she was the first and most perfect of Christ's disciples.' Notre Dame need look no further for its model of 'Catholic Character.'"

– Regina Coll, C.S.J.

"Our students come to us wanting to receive a first-rate education. We are bold enough to want to send them away closer to God."

– Terence H. Linton, C.S.C.

"...(A)mong the famous universities and colleges, it is the capacity for human decency that does distinguish us, that makes Notre Dame—and will ever make her—unique as a community of teachers and students, with the values of that community enduring with us and among us so long as life lasts."

– Frank O'Malley

"No matter what the moon of the hour, the University stands as a witness to the unseen; a sensitivity to 'beyondness' saturates these acres. The spirit is still held in high regard here.... Since a spirit of religion persists, it has always been easy to say yes to life at Notre Dame. While this place has known its cynics, it never developed a milieu in which cynicism was in and optimism was out. An affirmation of life is not considered corny on this campus. Perhaps that is why a blessing still lies on this place."

– Edward Fischer

"Reunions are a time to reconstruct the past. People and events are haloed with significance when seen from far off. Time's kindness puts a shine on things.

"...Under the circus tent that Saturday night there was enough drinking to soften the present, but still a miasma of sadness hung in the air. Things that pierce the memory deeply—old photo albums, old yearbooks, old hardships—bring an uneasy mirth. We laugh when we are reminded that God has the knack of planned obsolescence.

"Clustered in small groups on folding chairs, friends for many years took out memories and passed them around. The memories, blurred enough by now to be attractive, created a freemasonry that made us feel we still hold more in common than we really do. This was the time to enjoy the modified reminiscences of youth, not authenticate them. A stickler for facts is as out of place at an alumni reunion as Roman numerals on a scoreboard. Legends are not born in the midst of cross-references. And besides, to have delightful memories is to be written in the book of the blessed.

"...At a reunion, vivid camaraderie fades fast. The flow of reminiscence runs dry. The most garrulous is talked out. After a certain number of years, it takes courage to attend an alumni reunion. You face reflections of your mortality, seeing in others what is happening to yourself. It becomes more of a spiritual retreat than a lively celebration once you admit that not far downstream looms the Ultimate Tax Shelter. And yet those of us at the forty-fifth reunion said, 'See you at the fiftieth.' Such promises grow more chancy through the years.

"...We parted feeling more finite, knowing our horizons will move in like the wood of Dunsinane. In some well-worn classroom under the Dome we heard about 'this mortal coil,' but what did that mean at twenty? Now we don't need the bard, or anyone else, to tell us about mortality. Not if we were paying attention while the lessons were being taught.

" 'See you at the fiftieth!'

"With the permission of God, of course."

– Professor Edward Fischer

"A common burial ground will guard the ashes of the various members of the association. It is there that we shall await together, under the protection of the Cross, the hour of the final awakening.

For us who have the gift of faith, the ceme-

137

tery, which in our language means the sleeping place, is truly the spot for that rest which is a little longer than an ordinary night, and which will end with the radiant dawn of eternity."

– Fr. Basil Moreau, founder of the Congregation of Holy Cross

"Every time a sad report reaches our ears, let us remember the waves threatening the boat in which the Savior slept, and we will, as often, turn to Him and cry out from the depths of our hearts: 'Lord, save us lest we perish,' and He will awake and once more still the winds and the sea."

– Edward Sorin C.S.C.

"It ought to be clearly understood among us that in everything we should be governed not by private views or self-interest, but by principles."

– Fr. Edward Sorin, C.S.C.

"Look not to the number, but to the quality. Twelve men sufficed, in God's mind, to convert the world."

– Fr. Edward Sorin, C.S.C.

"The University looks best to me from some point midway between close up, where ordinary blemishes show, and far away where her distinctive beauty blurs."

– Ken Woodward, ND Alumnus and former Newsweek *writer*

"At the heart of everything we do here is the faith that anything is possible if you are willing to go in there and work harder. I would hate it if we ever lost that common touch, that concern about everyone here as an individual."

– Fr. Theodore Hesburgh, C.S.C.

"Father Ted had it right when he agonized over survival of the common touch that has characterized Notre Dame since it was still small enough, isolated enough and underrated enough to hold compassion as its core value. It remains so today; I can attest to that the way a veteran can attest to the true horror of war. I believe that there are many people at Notre Dame who want with all their hearts for that commitment to compassion to continue. But I can't be certain that the University will be able to do that, and fight the onslaught of rankings, hirings and unchecked aspirations that threaten the common touch, unless enough people come right out and say it should be so."

– Anthony dePalma

"It's o.k. to hear yourself praised as long as you don't inhale it. And, my dear friends, I'll try not to inhale."

– Fr. Hesburgh responding to speeches from the President and members of Congress as he received the Congressional Gold Medal in 2003

"I really believe that Our Lady watches over this place. I feel I ought to stop and say thanks, and also pray that she keeps watching over it. I usually get down there [to the Grotto] in the wee hours of the morning when I leave the office. There is almost always someone down there... rain, sleet or snow. Every university has a place where students hang out for their social life, libraries where they study, and fields where they play sports. But how many have a praying place?"

– Fr. Theodore Hesburgh, C.S.C.

"Hearts are comforted, lives are changed, and real miracles continue to happen. Faith is at the very heart of this University's life and mission, and the Grotto is at the very heart of Notre Dame."

– Most Rev. Daniel Jenky, former Rector of the Basilica of the Sacred Heart and now Bishop of Peoria, Illinois

"NOTRE DAME IS…
Home. A place where young spirits and hope
   soar,
and hope flames brightly on faces and in hearts,
where consolation and healing await the weary,
a place where sorrow and self doubt, failure and
loss can be brought to the railing at the Grotto
and entrusted to the Lady who stands watch over
all who come there."

"Notre Dame is a Holy Site to people who
never lived here or studied here, but in some real
and mysterious way, let it have a place in their
life. For some, it is a sign, a goal, a tabernacle, a
favorite place (even though unvisited), a destination. For Catholics it stands as proof of a coming
of age in America, against the odds, in the face of
intolerance, with no lessening of faith.

"A Font of Grace. Almost as if it is a field of
favor, this place takes hold, sometimes even of
the most recalcitrant, and removes the scales
from eyes so they can see again—or maybe for
the first time—with the vision of faith. Miracles
happen here—little ones and big ones—insights,
decisions, acceptance, rejuvenation, teased out
by some power that reaches the mind and soul.
Hardness of heart finds no easy home here;
magnanimity, bigness of soul, is in the land

142

and landscape. The graves of the unsung heroes who built the place, brick by brick, who cleaned and baked, cooked and cared, are nearby and somehow the spirit of giving all for the common good is in the air breathed here, a legacy that emanates from those who were here before us and that, with our touches added, will be here for those who come after us, for all time.

"Classrooms with a crucifix on the wall, a silent reminder that knowledge and truth need to culminate in goodness. Preparation for life, not simply for a profession happens here; there is no such thing as Catholic chemistry, but there is such a thing as a worldview that sees all of nature through eyes of faith and so catches nuances and tones that do not distort the picture; they simply make it whole.

"Notre Dame is Father Hesburgh making the University home for European intellectuals fleeing communism, or welcoming Monsignor Jack Egan, the great social justice activist, when his work was curtailed by the Archbishop of Chicago. Once, when I published at Notre Dame Press a book critical of Cardinal Cody and it brought episcopal wrath to Fr. Ted's door, I offered to resign. Fr. Ted sent me a note saying simply, 'We don't punish people at Notre Dame for responsible use of free speech.'

143

"People, generation after generations of them, here to study, write, teach, pray, work; privileged to be in the company of other searchers in a place dedicated to Mary, the Mother of Jesus. It is a family and it can trace its immediate lineage back to 1842, and its real ancestry back more than two millennia. Like every family, it has its share of dysfunction. Unlike every family, it also has the resources and the will to act in the best interest of the individual and the community as a whole. It is possible that there is no place on earth with a greater concentration of good people. No one who comes here seeking solace, inspiration, knowledge or care leaves unchanged. Like it or not, sense it or not, to come here is to be touched by and to take away some portion of the grace that seems to spring from the very ground. Not to worry; the supply is infinite.

"Memories shared by alumni, staff, and faculty, active and emeriti, of friends and friendships, of dorm life and homesickness, of dances and pep rallies, of the lakes and the lights on the dome, of Masses that uplifted, teachers who inspired, of talks long and deep that probed the very mystery of life. Physical presence here might now seem only a snapshot in time, like the photos of the South Quad filled with the formation of men in uniform training for battle during World War II, or earlier, the pictures of young men standing on campus next to unicycles brought back from Europe by Father Sorin. The spots where they stood are still there, still identifiable. You can still stand where Knute Rockne did when he was baptized in the Log Chapel on November 20, 1925. Or where his casket rested in Sacred Heart Church.

"Some day people will look at images of those on campus now and pause for a moment to marvel not at the changes, but at the continuity. No one who has ever walked near the Dome at night will forget how little and how large it made them feel just to be there. The statue of Father Sorin faces toward Notre Dame Avenue so that he can welcome his sons and daughters home again."

– Jim Langford '59

"My friends, our religion, our faith, does not take us out of life, but energizes and gives meaning to everyday life. It links us in solidarity to a community that stretches back 2,000 years....It has been sustained by men and women such as yourselves—the merciful, the single-hearted, the peacemakers. Dear friends, keep the faith, and in so doing live it and share it."

– Fr. Bill Miscamble, C.S.C., Professor of History

"Your years at Notre Dame have expanded both mind and heart. Your well-honed gifts will act as a beacon of hope for those you serve, and in turn, you will receive more blessings than you give."

– Fr. Mark Poorman, C.S.C.,
former Vice President for Student Affairs

"Notre Dame is more than an institution. Notre Dame is a way of life."

– Anonymous

"Some of us may not see many, even another new year; neither age nor vigor will avail, but a holy life will enable us to look steadfastly upon death as a deliverer from temptation and misery, holding out the crown promised to those who shall have persevered to the end."

– Fr. Edward Sorin, C.S.C.

"Son, in thirty-five years of religious study, I have only come up with two hard, incontrovertible facts: there is a God, and I am not him."

– Fr. John Cavanaugh, C.S.C. in Rudy

"Notre Dame, like families and graveyards, is all about communing across time and the hallowing of place."

– Kenneth Woodward '57

"Knowledge may be its own end in contemplation, but knowledge is also at the service of life in all of its manifestations. At the last, we shall all be judged on the charity in our hearts."

– Fr. Nicholas Ayo, C.S.C.

"The credentials of life are virtues we all recognize when we see them: goodness, competence, creativity, generosity, and dedication to truth and to compassionate humanity."

– Nicholas Ayo, C.S.C.

In 1972, after 125 years of all-male education, Notre Dame went coed. Sister Jean Lenz, O.F.M., was the first rector of Farley Hall when it was converted to house women. For nearly four decades now, Sr. Jean has been in the forefront of the ever-increasing presence and role of women at Notre Dame. She became famous for her "grow up, grow deep" talk to her charges over the years. She recalls:

"But my days in Farley brought me some of my deepest living experiences I have known in a lifetime. A generation ahead of the first Farley women, I simply moved into their midst and opened my door. They came in, questioned me incessantly on endless topics, picked my brain, and searched my heart, asking me to share my wisdom. They let me confront them with strong words and congratulate them with deep joy.

"We laughed and cried and discussed and danced and argued and ate and cheered together. We prayed together and forgave one another. They let me worry about them. Best of all they let me believe in them."

– *Sister Jean Lenz, O.F.M.*

"There's a special delight in watching parents recognize unselfishness in so many of their offspring, an amazing grace at work. It starts at home, becomes implanted there, and increases and multiplies. One mother confided that the most important things that happened to her daughter at Notre Dame began when she volunteered at Logan Center. As a visitor, this mother watched in amazement as her daughter moved with grace and ease among physically and mentally challenged children and young adults. And her daughter had no second thoughts about what this work meant to her. 'My Logan days gave focus to my whole education.'"

– Sr. Jean Lenz, O.S.F.

"Our lives are a 'Divine Comedy,' a love story with a happy ending. No matter the foolishness along the way, God is not finished with us yet. Thank God!"

– Fr. Nicholas Ayo, C.S.C.

"So, yes, I have optimism. There are just too many good people. Recent history is showing a drive for human dignity and a compassion for the Earth and all her creatures. There remains also a God of extraordinary compassion, kindness and justice. Love always wins...always!"

– Fr. Herb Yost, C.S.C.

"Yet the great miracle is not that we believe in God. Who else can we go to that still has credibility? The great miracle is that God still believes in us! We do so many crazy, stupid, irrational things, and yet God keeps believing in us and calling us to build a better world. There is no time to waste. We are, all of us, called to walk with God in our homes, in public, in the workplace, and, yes, on the streets."

– Notre Dame theologian Fr. Virgil Elizondo

"But it is God's reputation that He tracks down people because in some mysterious way, God needs each of us and all of us. Sinful and fickle as we are, we are His family, and God will leave the ninety-nine good sheep to search for the lost one. Most of us don't hear God calling us by name. But God knows where we are better than we do and accommodates our manner of knowing by sending both signs and the software necessary to read them."

– Jim Langford, Emeritus faculty, Notre Dame

"I felt free to call on the Holy Spirit because I never allowed that prayer was a way to avoid doing homework. Before you can offer a good answer to a pressing problem, you need to have a clear understanding of the problem itself and then to make certain you foresee the ramifications of the solution you propose. Principles can be perfectly true in the abstract, but more than a little complicated as they are applied to concrete problems....

"I never stopped studying on my journey through life. Whether the subject matter was higher education, social justice, atomic energy, peace or poverty, I felt an obligation to learn everything I could from whatever source..."

– Fr. Theodore M. Hesburgh, C.S.C.

"What I hope my life may have to say, especially to the young, is this: He believed, he hoped, he tried, he failed often enough, but with God's grace, he accomplished more than he rationally could have dreamed. He gave witness to those wonderful words of Scripture: 'God has chosen the weak of the world to confound the strong.' So we are weak. No matter."

– Fr. Theodore M. Hesburgh, C.S.C.

"Values are exemplified better than they are taught, which is to say that they are taught better by exemplification than by words."

– *Fr. Theodore M. Hesburgh, C.S.C.*

"If the vision of this institution is special and unique, it is because we cherish faith and values. Absent or present both of them, education and life are different."

– *Fr. Theodore M. Hesburgh, C.S.C.*

"The days ahead will also have their lessons, some easily and joyfully learned, and some that will etch your very souls in the strong acid of sorrow and adversity. We trust that the values you have learned here: the joy of truth, the exhilaration of beauty, the strength of goodness, the passion for justice, the quiet courage born of prayer, the love and compassion we owe our fellow men, the modesty and humility that our human frailty dictates, the reverence for the inner dignity of all things truly human, for human life from its beginning to its end—we trust that all

152

of these intellectual and moral qualities will take deeper root in you throughout all the days ahead, to enrich you as a person and to add luminosity to your life in a world often dark."

– Fr. Theodore Hesburgh, C.S.C.,
to the graduating class in 1987

"I entered my freshman year at Notre Dame skeptical that I would find God and suspicious of anyone who had found God. But my defensive walls were quickly surmounted by thoughtful peers, many of whom came from Catholic prep schools and knew more about Catholicism than I did, but who were seekers like me; classes that integrated church teaching with modern questions and problems; and a dorm life that included chapel, prayer, communion and community, spiritual growth and social outreach opportunities that became more and more appealing as I worked to understand who I was, who God is, and what this life is all about."

– Jeremy Langford '92

"I have heard that the campus is a Catholic Disneyland, but I have never heard that Notre Dame is the Kingdom of God on Earth or the Garden of Paradise. We know that there is a mixture of virtue and sin, of good and bad, of fair and unfair on this campus. We are in the world even if we wish not to be of the world. No one here is without sin. Humility befits us, and patience. We are an unfinished story. One has but to read the history of Notre Dame and the many-sided conflict between Fr. Edward Sorin, C.S.C., as founder of the University, and Fr. Basil Moreau, C.S.C., founder of the Congregation of Holy Cross, to recognize that our roots, our motives, our virtues and our vices are all entangled and that only God in the end time will fully sort out our days. In the meantime, we bear each others' burdens and we like to think at Notre Dame we do so with some humor and some willingness to carry more than our share on occasion. Who of us would write our autobiography today in just the same way we would have as a student at Notre Dame? Some weeds back then turned out to be wheat, and some wheat back then turned out to be weeds. We think we know what is good and what is bad for us, but we are not infallible judges of the Providence of God."

– Fr. Nicholas Ayo, C.S.C.

"Human life might be described as our many goodbyes. Sooner or later we must say goodbye to most everyone we have known. We say goodbye to classmates as we graduate, to family when we leave home, indeed, to the world itself when we come to die. Just as all things in this life break, so too, all people in our lives are parted from us. We also say our goodbyes to lost dreams, lost loves, lost friends, lost choices. We have lost alums at Notre Dame whom we cannot trace or find. Betrayals by State or Church, by home or school, broken promises and cruel words can all lead to losing and being lost. Alumni reunions have some success, but we often find them occasions to share our losses with others in the same boat. Springtime flowers and flowering trees at Notre Dame seem perfect and unspoiled, when leaves are fresh, green, clean and without bug attacks. Then there is a long hot summer, and we know lost innocence in that recurrent heat, even as we do believe we will all meet again in the resurrection of the body and life everlasting."

– Fr. Nicholas Ayo, C.S.C.

Of Notre Dame students, Fr. Hesburgh said:

"I don't know how they get it, but they get it like three minutes after they get here—it's like a contagion for good in the air—and somehow they become bonded to this place immediately. One of the trustees used to say that this was the highest concentration of goodness of any place on earth. I wouldn't make that boast—it's a little much. But today we do all stand in a special spot, and it's a special spot because it's guarded over by the Mother of God."

"The campus is ablaze with light in every growing thing and in every radiant person made in the image of God. It may not be a stretch to see the campus as a garden of God's own making, through our own shaping of it, sometimes more and sometimes less than we had hoped."

– *Fr. Nicholas Ayo, C.S.C.*

"Notre Dame is a magic place: small enough to reach in and touch your soul, large enough to extend your reach around the world."

– *Author unknown*

"In the shadow of the Golden Dome,
tucked in a wooded hillside,
there is light.
A beacon of comfort for one
hundred years, the Grotto is
at the heart of Notre Dame.
At this rocky shrine to Mary,
the Mother of God,
in an idyllic lakeside setting,
lives are quietly touched.
Countless of the faithful have
brought their burdens and
their thanks to the Grotto,
lit a candle to prolong a prayer...
found peace."

– Mary Trish Dowling

"Incidentally, it is the lack of love in a person's
life which Mother Teresa insists is the greatest
poverty of all. Far more devastating than hunger
for food is hunger for love. Far more saddening
than poverty of body is poverty of spirit. The
poor live in a powerless and dependent world
and many feel insignificant, unimportant and
unwanted. Even the smallest gesture of love can
bring more to their lonely world than we could
ever understand."

*– Lou Nanni, Vice-President for
University Relations, Notre Dame*

Declan

By Amy Holsinger '12

I did not know Declan Sullivan.

On Wednesday, Declan was killed on campus in an accident involving a hydraulic lift. He was filming football practice for his job as a student manager, and high winds caused the scissor lift he was filming from to topple over.

He was 20 years old. He was a junior majoring in FTT (film, television, and theater) and marketing. He lived in Fisher Hall.

Tonight, Father John Jenkins, University President, presided over a Mass in Declan's memory in the Basilica of the Sacred Heart.

Mass began at 10 p.m. I was in a lecture and movie screening for class until 9:45 p.m., and I wasn't sure if I was going to make it to the Basilica in time to get a seat. I also wasn't sure if I even wanted to go to the Mass. I didn't know Declan, so a part of me thought, "Why should I take a seat from somebody who knew him, loved him, cared about him? Who am I to do that?" But another part of me desperately wanted to go to the Mass to show my support for Declan's family during this horrible, difficult time. That part of me wanted to show the Sullivans that Notre Dame is a place where everybody matters, a place where the spirit of the community links everybody together. I was already running late and I knew that my baseball-cap-and-Ugg-boot attire wouldn't fly at the Basilica, so I decided to go over to LaFortune Student Center, where I had heard there would be auxiliary seating and a live feed from the Mass.

As I walked across God Quad in the dark, I watched people walking towards the Basilica, two by two. The doors were wide open, emanating a warm golden glow. I was able to hear the prelude for Declan's Mass all the way at the flagpole on South Quad, and the sound of the organ became clearer as I crossed through the pine trees and made my way to LaFortune.

Up the winding staircase, I burst into LaFortune and brushed past the representatives from the Student Activities Office who tried to usher me upstairs to the ballroom. "We have some seats left up there," a girl with a nametag whispered. By the time I heard her, I had already set down my backpack near my usual spot in the main lounge. LaFortune was different. Normally, the building serves as a study/food/coffee/socialization/meeting space, and it's one of the busiest places on campus. But tonight, it was quiet. Dimmer, somehow.

All of the comfy armchairs were occupied,

so after lingering against a wall, cornered by a trashcan, for a few minutes, I plopped down on the floor like a kindergartener. Mass was beginning. The broadcast was coming through on the two large televisions in the main lounge. (It was available online as well.) During the opening song, the SAO folks brought out a number of chairs from another room, and I snapped up a seat just as Fr. Jenkins was greeting the Sullivan family.

Then, the oddest thing began to happen. Everyone in the room began to respond to the TV, just like Mass.

Peace be with you.

"And also with you."

I don't know if it was reflex, a genuine desire to participate in the Mass, or some combination of both. All of a sudden, I found myself in the midst of the celebration of the Eucharist in the same room where I drink coffee, read the paper, watch ESPN, and play Sporcle.

Notre Dame is very good at a lot of things, and one of those things is church. Notre Dame knows how to put on a great Mass, and the higher-ups pulled out all the stops for Declan. The Folk Choir provided beautiful music for the service. I was particularly impressed with the selection of the readings. The first reading was

Romans 8:31-39 ("If God is for us, who can be against us?"). The gospel reading was John 14:1-14 ("I am the way and the truth and the life. No one comes to the Father except through me.").

Father Tom Doyle, Vice President for Student Affairs, gave the homily. He spoke eloquently and simply about storytelling—about Declan's love of telling stories through film and about the feeling that we have been "written out of the book of life" that accompanies loss and grief. Doyle said, "Most days, we live in this place that is like Eden before the fall." Normally, bad things don't happen here. Students joke about the "Notre Dame bubble" for a reason. When terrible things hit Notre Dame, it seems that much worse.

As I watched the Mass on TV from my chair in LaFortune, I noticed that the camera kept panning out to the people sitting in the pews at the Basilica. The Sullivan family sat in the front row. Gwyneth, Declan's sister, wore a Notre Dame football jersey and Mac, Declan's 15-year-old brother, wore a Notre Dame sweatshirt. Across the aisle, the men of Fisher Hall sat in the other front section, all with their trademark neon green retro sunglasses pushed back into messy brown waves and perched on blonde crew cuts. Fisher men wear these distinguishing sunglasses around campus all the time, so it seemed appropriate that they wore their shades to Mass in memory of their hall mate. The Notre Dame football team sat behind the contingent from Fisher Hall.

During the Eucharistic Prayer, LaFortune was filled with the mutterings of hundreds of students.

Lift up your hearts.

"We lift them up to the Lord."

When it came time for the Our Father, the Folk Choir sang the beautiful Notre Dame Our Father. LaFortune joined hands and joined in. Then, everyone got out of their seats for the sign of peace. Hugs and handshakes all around.

The SAO employees notified us that the Eucharist was being distributed outside the Basilica and that we could leave and come back. After a moment of hesitation, about 75 percent of the room stood up, grabbed coats, and quietly filed out of the room. I was near the door, so I made it out quickly. Down the stairs, across the quad, towards the music and light. There were hundreds of people already standing outside the Basilica—overflow. Outside, there were musicians performing acoustic versions of the songs playing inside. As I huddled around the front of the Basilica, I turned around. A massive block of students stretched all the way from the foot of the Basilica to the stairs of LaFortune, and people continued to stream out of the building from the ballroom on the second floor.

We stood patiently, quietly in the cold. Occasionally, a priest would emerge from the big Basilica doors. People gathered around eagerly as the priest distributed Communion. Nobody jostled, nobody complained. We just waited. Slowly, more priests came out. After I received Communion, I walked back to LaFortune. I counted six priests standing outside, each man completely surrounded by students waiting for the Eucharist.

I made it back to LaFortune just in time for the final blessing.

The Mass is ended, go in peace to love and serve the Lord.

"Thanks be to God."

And then, as always, we sang the alma mater, arms around each other, swaying.

Notre Dame, Our Mother
Tender, strong and true
Proudly in the heavens
Gleams thy gold and blue.
Glory's mantle cloaks thee
Golden is thy fame.
And our hearts forever
Praise thee, Notre Dame.
And our hearts forever
Love thee, Notre Dame.

The fervent prayers of the Notre Dame community are with Declan Sullivan and his family. A night like this should never have to happen again.

"Notre Dame is in my bones for sure. I have a deep passion about the school itself...not just the football program. The standard the university teaches regarding life and how to approach it with dignity is something that seems to be lost in our society today. I became a true fan of ND when I was 10...my father Pastored a church in Cumberland, MD, at the time and I went to a slumber party with a friend from school. The next day (Saturday) all the girls were still asleep, but I was up. I went downstairs and the family of the home that the slumber party was held at were avid ND fans...I watched the pre-game show and when I saw the tradition and dignity, passion and reverence the players and the school exuded...my ND passion was born.

"The sacredness of a thing is something to be cherished. However, I find fewer and fewer things that are in a caliber of 'sacred' these days, but Notre Dame holds true to sacredness with their respect and honor. In life there are so many disappointments...but when Notre Dame plays and even if we lose badly...ND still isn't a disappointment. The concept of "The Fighting Irish" is one of the best things I embedded in my mind as a kid. When life or an adversary unapologetically beats you to a pulp, leaving you blind, doesn't back up or let up...it's a reminder to still fight... don't give in...don't give up. Get up and fight.

"We're all here for a time...we only occupy the land or homes that we buy. It's not really ours. Material things do not matter—what other people think does not matter...what does matter is what a person is accountable for in their deeds, actions, words and character. To make an existence relevant...to fight for something that's greater and bigger than your own soul is to me the most sacred showing of character.

"We Are The Fighting Irish!"

– Bessie C. Ross

(*Bessie Ross is a prime example of the thousands of people across this country who, even without having attended Notre Dame, or without ever having seen its campus in person, has adopted the school and imbibed its spirit, initially because as a youngster she met people who embodied Notre Dame.*)

"Teaching, caring, touching lives, knowing the importance of people. The human touch. And knowing that Notre Dame means taking care of people, taking the time to care, and that there is something about the whole enterprise, the community, the legacy and traditions, that transcends the individual, the moment in time, that is bigger than any one person, and yet calls upon each person to extend the reach, to spread the inheritance. Throughout its history, Notre Dame has been enriched by this generosity of spirit, has befriended generations with a kindness of heart. The Notre Dame family is no myth."

– Kerry Temple '74

FACT: One of the most popular holidays in America is Mother's Day. Its founder is Notre Dame graduate Frank E. Herring who, in a speech before the Fraternal Order of Eagles Convention on February 7, 1904, urged that one day a year be set aside for special recognition of motherhood. Needless to say, the idea caught on!

"When you walked you were surrounded by the place, by an atmosphere, by a whole embracing, exciting, confirming tradition. Down a flight of stairs, around a bend, in the hall chapel, there was God."

— *Richard Sullivan*

"I have been here long enough now to have seen a lot of the place, to have been disappointed in its human frailties, to have moved far beyond the rosy patina of memory, romance and sentiment. But when I have become disillusioned or grumpy, when I have witnessed too much of the politics and personalities, I take a walk. And the campus, the very place itself, welcomes me as it did so many years ago. I have only to walk the lakes or sit alone at the Grotto or rest on a bench and watch awhile in order for the place to show itself again, to reside in me, to work its spell again. And I know then that there is something here, something about the place, something within the landscape itself, that transcends the human, that sustains the promise and the legacy, that suggests the smile of God."

— *Kerry Temple '74*

"LOGAN is just one of many community organizations here in South Bend and around the country that benefit from the results of the Notre Dame spirit of service...These Notre Dame service projects put the spirit of the message into action. As valuable as teaching, research and striving to excel in athletics all are, the spirit of Notre Dame is service."

– Dan Harshman, ND alumnus; former football player at ND; CEO, LOGAN: Resources and Opportunities for People with Disabilities

"As a young Irish Catholic growing up in the coal regions of Northeastern Pennsylvania, I was drawn to Notre Dame as a youngster; a neighbor gave me an early copy of *Blue & Gold Illustrated* and I was sold. Notre Dame, much like where I grew up, is a place where it is all right to be Catholic, a place that you can gather and say the Rosary in good times and in bad.

"In these times when our past seems to be forgotten, what keeps me tuned in to the Notre Dame spirit are the simple things, a smile and nod from a priest, ordering a meat-free meal on a Friday and not being looked at funny.

"What started out as a young boy loving a

football team has grown into a desire to live my life in a way that represents very core values of Notre Dame—compassion and forgiveness leading that list.

"I live my life today by keeping things simple; this is why the Father Langes and Mario Tonellis have a special place in my heart. Sometimes the lesser-known stories are the greatest."

– *Jim Sheridan*

"As many will recall, there are days—many days—in the late fall when it starts to get cold and wet in South Bend and you keep your head down while crossing the quiet campus at night, maybe on the way back from another dorm or The Huddle or on the way to the library. It is so harsh out that you don't notice the big Jesus on the library or, if this was your era, even notice that Hesburgh's light is on. You mutter to yourself about how your friends at other schools are warmer, have more to do. You think of transferring, going where brighter lights are. Then from a far corner of the campus by the stadium you hear it: the band is finishing up practice over by that House That Rockne Built and it's coming your way in the dark. It's the Victory March they

169

are playing and it's coming right toward you, getting louder. There is no one near you, and suddenly you're a kid again. You walk faster and you're not cold anymore. Your spirit is changed. Everything you want is right there."

– Bill Gunlocke, ND alumnus and founding editor of A City Reader *in NYC*

"Notre Dame people are not complacent; they are afraid of complacency. But they are not afraid or ashamed of enthusiasm. They are capable of being enthusiasts in the deepest literal sense."

– Professor Stephen Rodgers

"...Some refer to the 1970s as part of Notre Dame's glory years. I would agree. It was a special time in a different way, too, because of guys like Al Sondej.

"He was a tall muscular fellow, who stood outside the North Dining Hall every day with a milk jug, as I recall, asking students for spare change.

"At first, he seemed creepy. It didn't look right for a student at a private university to be panhandling.

"And for the first few weeks, we freshmen would all avoid him. We would use a different entrance, sneak out a different exit.

"It took us a while to realize Big Al wasn't going to go away.

"If you plunked a couple of dimes into his jug, he would thank you. If you just walked by, he would nod anyway.

"If you asked, and some people did, he would tell you that he was raising money for Third World Hunger Relief.

By the time he graduated in 1974, he had raised $25,000, a dime here and a quarter there.

"He also had told thousands of young men and women at this white, Catholic, upper-middle-class school about starving people with different skin colors, with different religious beliefs, on different continents."

– Ken Bradford '76

(A volunteer fireman, Al Sondej died in 1988 of burns sustained attempting a rescue in a burning building.)

"That is what makes Notre Dame such a different kind of place. Those fortunate enough to come here are not merely fed, they are nourished. Mentally, physically, emotionally and spiritually

we are nourished. The totality of one's person-
hood is attended to here. Few places in the world
do that."

– Fr. William Seetch, C.S.C., Notre Dame

"Steadfastness in devotions every day makes one
mindful that no matter what pressures or delib-
erations have to be faced, they have behind them
a will and care firmly rooted in the love of God
and humankind, and a commitment that comes
from deep within one's own identity."

– Fr. Theodore Hesburgh, C.S.C.

"One grave danger of college is if education is
seen (and designed) principally as a preparation
for making a living instead of a preparation for
life. It can function for gain, not for growth.

"In many universities the humanities don't
humanize, they neutralize. Students are asked
the wrong question—'When you graduate, what
are you going to do?' whereas the real question
is: 'When you graduate, what are you going to
be?' The chief concern should be what kind of
person you will become."

– Fr. Bill Toohey, C.S.C.

"A mountain climber was high on a mountain and he fell. Fortunately, he grabbed a bush growing out of the mountainside and hung there with his feet dangling in space, hundreds of feet above ground. He called to his friend below for help, but the friend couldn't get to him.

"He then called out to anyone above for help. 'Is there anyone up there?' A voice from above answered, 'I am here.' 'Who are you?' said the climber. 'I am God,' came the answer. The man was overjoyed and asked for help. God said, 'I will help you, but first you will have to do what I tell you.' 'Anything, anything at all,' replied the climber. Then God said, 'Let go of the bush.' There was a long silence from the climber; then the man yelled out, 'Is there anyone *else* up there?'

"That story says a lot about faith. We find faith tough. By it God seems to demand the impossible: He keeps saying, 'Let go of the bush.' "

– *Fr. Bill Toohey, C.S.C.*

"The gospel is not a pill to help us avoid the pain of life, but a revelation that shows the way to transform something into the birth pangs of something new."

– *Fr. Bill Toohey, C.S.C.*

"I have for some time now been a chaplain of the Notre Dame team. I'm getting to dread each and every game. That's when countless people begin to say things like: 'Well, your prayers really worked today, Father!' or 'You better pray extra hard for this one!' or 'What happened?! Looks like you didn't say the right words!'

"When my prayers 'work,' as, say in the famous Sugar Bowl victory over Alabama, what am I supposed to think? That the prayers of the Alabama fans didn't work? The God I believe in doesn't cause fumbles, help with tackles, influence passes, and his Mother doesn't specialize in guiding ND Field goals through the uprights. God doesn't win football games. Men win games. God's desire is to win men."

– *Fr. Bill Toohey, C.S.C.*

"Love means a lot to me, because I see so much of it in my work in campus ministry. I see much of it every day; and some days are specially filled with love's dimensions. For example, during last school year I went to Dayton, Ohio, to attend the funeral of one of our students, who was killed in a tragic automobile accident. I saw many manifestations of love on that occasion. I found out what love means. Love means—well, it means a mother and a father who are torn with pain over the death of their oldest son, and yet can think only of being gracious and kind and sensitive to the needs of others, wonderfully hospitable to the relatives and friends who were with them on that occasion. Love means—well, love means the grandmother of this student, herself dying of cancer, yet the most outgoing, energetic, least self-pitying person in the crowd. Love means three carloads of Notre Dame students, who got up at four-thirty on a winter morning and drove through a northern Indiana blizzard to participate in the funeral Mass and burial of their friend.

"The song is right: 'What the world needs now is love, sweet love; that's the only thing that there's just too little of.' But it seems there's more to it than that. Although there is indeed a lack of love—such a tremendous need for more love in this world—there are also, if we look at the total picture, fantastic demonstrations and manifestations of love around us all the time. We ought to see this. We ought to rejoice in it, thank God for it...recognize him in it. For, after all, love is his name."

– Fr. Bill Toohey, C.S.C.

"Dear God,
Thank you for the gifts
of so many socially concerned persons,
past, present, and future,
sharing in your mission to work
toward a more humane and just world.

Gracias for the ND Alums
and other committed persons
who welcome students to serve and learn
in areas of great human need—
Urban Plunges, Summer Service Projects,
Break Seminars...

Thank you for the willingness
of those suffering AIDS, poverty, injustice,
oppression, and homelessness
to be our teachers and to challenge us
to 'Do the Truth in Love.'

Gracias for the privilege
of being blessed and challenged
over many years
by stories, books, witnesses, reflections
and prayers of men and women
of Notre Dame
whose compassion is rooted
in you and your grace. Amen."

– Fr. Don McNeill, C.S.C., Former Director of the
Center for Social Concerns, Notre Dame

"If Jesus always calmed our storms, we could very easily look upon him as a sort of Mister Fixit. We might turn our attention away from his person and be principally concerned with what he could do for us...It is hard for us to understand why he makes it hard for us to follow, why he refuses to be a folk hero, why he will not give us the signs and credentials which would make it so much easier for us...The only true credentials are the signs given by the faith of others who have the courage and daring to surrender to Christ without credentials. It comes down to this: we are called to stand with Jesus, not because we have nothing better to do, but because there *is* nothing better to do."

– Fr. Bill Toohey, C.S.C.

"At its best, my faith reflects the qualities—doubt, fear, passion, intensity, trust, courage, hope, grief—that are preoccupying the students, children, colleagues and friends of the Notre Dame community. For, as a Christian, I am here not only to witness to faith, but also to find it incarnate in the heartbeats that dance to the rhythms of grace."

– Fr. Robert Griffin, C.S.C.

"We need to shine our light of invitation as brightly as possible, aiming it squarely into the darkest recesses of ignorance or hopelessness. We need to cultivate the gifts that this Spirit of Notre Dame gives us... And then we need to do what Notre Dame does best—to go out and share stories about the relationships, the lessons, the places and the legacies that still call out to pilgrims like us."

– Fr. John Jenkins, C.S.C.,
President of Notre Dame

"Faithfulness to its roots and its mission requires that this be a place where the Church does its thinking, where there is constant effort to understand and teach what it means to be a Christian in the contemporary world. Fidelity is not a hurdle to creativity; instead, it is a touchstone: it helps ground us in what we stand for and what we won't stand for."

– Fr. Theodore Hesburgh, C.S.C.,
President Emeritus

"If you want to belong, you have to learn the myth. You have to wrap your heart and mind in it. You have to believe that the merest rocks of the place tell a story... Behind the myths is a cast of hundreds working in loyalty for the Notre Dame of their dreams, in a love affair that lasts a lifetime."

– *Fr. Robert Griffin, C.S.C.*

"As an undergrad senior at ND in 1970-71, trying to decide what to do with my life and career, I decided to dedicate my life to ND in some way because, as I thought at the time, 'It is the finest institution *I'll* ever have anything to do with.'

"Now, as a 31-year senior faculty member, I see it this way: ND is a unique institution because of the rare combinations it tries to achieve. First, it is one school that is truly and genuinely dedicated to undergrad teaching while being fully committed to research. Even more fundamentally, ND endeavors to be a great academic institution while not sacrificing its Catholic character. For those reasons, I was right from the beginning: ND is a very admirable institution. It has earned the dedication and love that people bestow upon it."

– *Professor John Gaski, Notre Dame*

"From my early days here, I was witness not only to the responses of the 'Notre Dame Family' to the joys of colleagues but also, more significantly, to their tragedies, exemplified by a young Indian scientist who lost his wife through cancer. A delegation of faculty wives took care of his children and the running of the household until he recovered from that shocking experience. A faculty member suffered a stroke in Florida: the University brought him home by private jet. Students were killed in an accident: members of the faculty visited the homes of the students to console their families. An employee needed an immediate blood transfusion: blood donors came from all segments of the Notre Dame family. When tragedy strikes, this family does respond."

— Dr. Morris Pollard, Emeritus Professor,
Director Emeritus of the Lobund Laboratory

"I cannot encapsulate here all that the University of Notre Dame has meant to me and to my life. I can only try by repeating one sentence I spoke from the heart in my valedictory address:

"'To have been president of such a company of valiant searching souls, to have shared with you: the peace, the mystery, the optimism, the *joie de vivre*, the ongoing challenge, the ever youthful ebullient vitality, and, most of all, the deep and abiding caring that characterize this special place and all of its people, young and old, this is a blessing that I hope to carry with me into eternity when that time comes.' "

– Fr. Theodore Hesburgh, C.S.C.,
President Emeritus, Notre Dame

"My Notre Dame experience changed my life. It's not just the victories, it's the perspective on life you receive there. For example, the first thing we did after winning the National Championship was to have Mass—before we celebrated, before we met with our friends and family. Lou Holtz himself delivered the homily. That showed all of us there are more important things in life."

– Reggie Ho

(best remembered as the 5'5" placekicker on the 1988 Irish Championship team)

"The life of a Notre Dame alumnus should typify commitment. A person who does not seek to grow spiritually is not a Notre Dame alumnus.

A person who does not seek to act morally is not a Notre Dame alumnus. A man who is afraid to confront old problems with new ideas, who is afraid to confront himself, has wasted four years at Notre Dame."

– Gary Caruso, speech to ND Alumni Board, 1970

Notre Dame's esteemed Rev. Louis Putz, C.S.C., an unselfish giver throughout his entire adult life, once said that life consists of three stages: learning, earning, and returning. That would make Harry Durkin '53 a quintessential "third stager."

Whether organizing food drives, packing and sending care packages to the men and women serving in Iraq and Afghanistan, or distributing toys to the children of residents in local shelters, Durkin's commitment to community service is unmatched. As a salute to his generosity of time and spirit, the ND Club of Fort Lauderdale has named Durkin "Father of the Year."

A former president of the ND Club of Fort Lauderdale, Durkin has served on both the national Alumni Association Board of Directors and the Senior Alumni (NDSA) Board of Directors. As his club's incumbent Senior

Alumni coordinator, Durkin directs its out-reach programs. With his guidance, the club has prepared hundreds of food baskets for disadvantaged families as part of the Holy Cross Thanksgiving Food Drive; it built a new kitchen for the residents of Covenant House, an area shelter for battered women; and for 22 years, it has subsidized two ND students who volunteer for eight weeks each summer to mentor children at Covenant House.

A Message of Thanks

Fresh from their 2,200-mile bike ride of hope, Greg Crawford, William K. Warren Foundation Dean of the College of Science, and his wife, Renate, offer this message of gratitude to the Notre Dame family:

"It is impossible to describe the feeling we had riding down Notre Dame Avenue, completing our Desert to Dome trek on August 23. From our first experience with the University, we have known what a special community surrounds this place. And still, every day that we pushed to a new city or were welcomed by a new Notre Dame club, we continued to be astonished by the genuine love and staggering support we felt from the Notre Dame family. We have updated our blog with a highlights video (http://blogs.nd.edu/gregcrawford/video/), which captures memories we will cherish forever.

"The ride is now over, but it truly does seem like the journey is just beginning. We are—more than ever—committed to finding a cure for Niemann-Pick Type C (NPC) (http://niemannpick.nd.edu). With the University's new partnership with the Ara Parseghian Medical Research Foundation and the devoted support of the Notre Dame family, we are confident that we will win this fight and put an end to the heartbreak of NP-C.

Yours in Notre Dame,
Greg and Renate Crawford

Notre Dame is a place of learning, believing, hoping, resolving, befriending, consoling, challenging, seeking, growing, and renewing. One can almost touch the grace that abounds here. But it is also a place where fallibility has a foothold. It cannot rightly claim perfection in those who administer, teach, study or visit here. Rather, it needs to be accepted for what it is: a place where the pursuit of excellence is relentless in spite of failures, where the spirit invites one and all to witness to the miracles of grace in a world always in need of those miracles.

Basilica Interior – circa 1866-1924

ATHLETICS

"In fact, I sometimes feel that the alumni are impossible in their unfair demands for victory. I think it was Major Cavanaugh who once said that if he had his choice of coaching positions, and the salaries were all the same, he would like to coach at Sing Sing. 'The alumni very seldom come back, and when they do come back they are never noisy.'"

– Knute Rockne

"They [the Four Horsemen] comprised a wonderful backfield. I have never seen any better. But the line which played in front of them was a thing of beauty to watch and was justly entitled to half the credit."

– Knute Rockne

"Never ridicule a beginner—you can kill talent before it blossoms."

– Knute Rockne

"Someday there will be an exhibit in some American museum. It will be the forlorn figure of a coach who pleased nobody. And next to it will be another—and more forlorn exhibit—the preserved remains of the coach who tried to please everybody."

– Knute Rockne

"Of course, when the team wins everybody talks about 'we,' but when the team loses then they mention 'him,'—that's me."

– Knute Rockne

"Boys, there seems to be considerable dispute as to which part of the team is more important—the line or the backfield. I believe in settling such disputes in democratic fashion. So we'll take a vote on it. The line wins, seven votes to four. And don't you backs ever forget it."

– Knute Rockne

"Rockne taught us the basics; things like honesty, courage, the will to win. With Rock, the starting point was 100%. He was always looking for more than that and that's what we always tried to give him."

– Adam Walsh, All-American center, 1925

September 30, 1980...there are 10 seconds left in the hard-fought battle between ND and Michigan. ND has a fourth down on the Michigan 39 yard line. Coach Dan Devine calls on left-footed kicker Harry Oliver to try the longest field goal kick of his career...51 yards.

Oliver asks Tim Koegel, the holder, "What should I do?" Koegel's reply is not, "Win one for the Gipper." Instead he says, "Just kick the hell out of it and kick it straight." Oliver did: ND 29 Michigan 27. Defensive tackle Pat Kramer said it best, "This could only happen here."

– Jeff Jeffers

"You know what it takes to win. Just look at my fist. When I make a fist, it's strong and you can't tear it apart. As long as there's unity, there's strength. We must become so close with the bonds of loyalty and sacrifice, so deep with the conviction of the sole purpose, that no one, no group, no thing, can ever tear us apart."

– Ara Parseghian

From Frank Leahy:

- "Discipline is indispensable in the education of a gentleman."

• • • • •

- "Pay the price in sweat, effort and sacrifice and strive for perfection in each day's drill."

• • • • •

- "Egotism is the anesthetic that deadens the pain of stupidity."

(Also attributed to Knute Rockne)

• • • • •

- "Remember this, lads, never, never, never give up."

"We are in the first chapter of the book; it's a little tough to read right now, but I'd stick with the book."

– Coach Brian Kelly after the 2010 loss to Stanford
in his first season at the helm

"Should any Notre Dame team ever be so unfortunate as to post a 1-10 season, there is little doubt that most fans would want the lone victory to be over the University of Southern California."

– WNDU Sports Director Jeff Jeffers

"It really goes back to the summer, with lacrosse getting to the final game, and then the extraordinary run by the women's soccer team, and then fencing, and now we have women's basketball and hockey in finals," Swarbrick said. "You see that sometimes, because what happens is, student-athletes motivate each other. They see each other; they run into each other all the time. They change expectations of each other in a way that, frankly, coaches can't. That's what we're seeing now."

*– ND Athletic Director Jack Swarbrick
on the 2010-2011 success of Irish sports teams*

"The pride and tradition of Notre Dame football will not be left to the weak, the timid or the non-committed."

– Coach Brian Kelly

"Kelley Siemon came in from Virginia. LeTania Severe made it in from Florida. For Danielle Green, it was a trip from Chicago. Jackie Batteast led a caravan from South Bend. And for former Rochester star Sheila McMillen, it was an easy drive from her Indianapolis home.

In all, nearly 40 former Notre Dame women's basketball players were at Conseco Fieldhouse to cheer on the Irish....

"Seeing her former players in the stands was especially touching for [Coach Muffet] McGraw. 'That's one of the best parts,' McGraw said of reconnecting with Irish alums. 'I think after we beat Tennessee, I got texts and e-mails from former players and they were working on getting here for this game, and from so many different eras.

" 'When you're here as long as I've been here, there were people even before I got here that played back in the beginning and then all throughout the '97 team and the '80s and the '90s and the championship group and thereafter,' McGraw said. 'It's been amazing to see so many people come back and kind of relive those old stories and talk about things. But they're also proud. That's probably the biggest thing they've all said: 'I'm so proud to be a Notre Dame alum.' "

– *Coach McGraw (Reported by Curt Rollo)*

"...On November 10, 1928, only four days after Al Smith's humiliating defeat in the presidential election, Rockne managed one of the most celebrated Notre Dame football victories in history by beating Army 12 to 7 in Yankee Stadium before a crowd of 78,000. A headline from the *New York Herald Tribune* on November 11 summed up the anti-Catholic turmoil of the last several months by screaming, 'After the election came Rockne's revenge.'

"...A more likely source of the idea of using the memory of Gipp to inspire the Notre Dame team to play beyond themselves against a very strong West Point squad was one of [Grantland] Rice's colleagues on the *New York Herald Tribune*, W.O. McGeehan. On Friday, November 9, 1928, McGeehan treated his readers to a full laudatory column on 'Gipp of Notre Dame,' recounting Gipp's performance against Army in 1920 and describing him as the greatest football player he had ever watched. After describing Gipp's tragic and untimely death, McGeehan implied that his hero for this column had been a decent person, good citizen, and appropriate role model for the youth of the country. This extraordinary rehabilitation of Gipp's unsavory reputation as a gambler, pool shark, drinker, and utterly indifferent to academics by a celebrity sportswriter who should have known better was enough for Rockne. He proceeded to make use of Gipp's memory as he saw fit.

"At the end of the season, there was not much worth remembering except for the Army game. [ND won 5 and lost 4—at that point the worst record in modern ND history.] On that day against a superior Army team, inspired words persuasively delivered had transformed journeymen players into champions for an afternoon. This fact resonated throughout the American sports world in 1928 and continues to do so today. Ironically, Rockne's greatest athletic moment, now an established sports legend, occurred not during one of his best seasons but in his worst ever."

– Notre Dame historian Robert Burns

"Any time you don't do the best you're capable of, you're cheating yourself."

– Lou Holtz

"One, the team is more important than the individual. You have to subjugate your welfare for the sake of the team.

"Two, consistency is more important than greatness. I don't care how great a player can be, I want to know what to expect from you day to day.

"Three, it's a privilege to represent Notre Dame.

"Four, it's ability that determines your capability, but your attitude that dictates your performance.

"Five, we're going to select intelligent players who know what they're doing.

"Six, an individual who won't do it is no better than one who can't..."

– Lou Holtz, cited by John Heisler

"...(A)s soon as we are dressed, all of us are going to visit the cathedral to offer up a prayer of thanksgiving. Before you do any celebrating, send a telegram to your father and mother thanking them for the privilege of letting you play for Notre Dame."

– Coach Frank Leahy to his 1949 team
after they finished an undefeated
National Championship season
with a win over SMU

"That Rockne was bigger than life is true but some of the legendary stories about him are not. Many, I think, are fictitious. Professor Paul Fenlon, who knew Rockne in his man-about-campus days, once told me he asked him about one of his famous between-halves speeches. 'All I said,' Rockne told him, was 'watch Cagle'" [referring to Chris Cagle, a famous Army star].

— *Tom Stritch*

"Since I came to Notre Dame [in 1930] the football mystique has grown and grown, like Jack's beanstalk...I thought that the memory of Rockne would fade away, like that of matinee idols of the theater. But since World War II and Frank Leahy, I have come to believe that college football is one of the hardiest vessels of our civilization. And there is no doubt that Notre Dame is its flagship. I have seen the ship dead in the water in season after season of inept coaching, but each time new leadership has brought it back to lead the fleet."

— *Tom Stritch*

"Something he [Frank Leahy] said to me in the press box about half way through the first quarter of a football game we were watching after he stopped coaching is a good clue to his character. 'You know, Tom,' he said, 'that offensive line of ours has a good charge.' Then he breathed heavily and clenched his fist and added, 'But they don't do it every time!'"

– Tom Stritch

"You take over a new company as the CEO, and you're having a rough quarter. You're going, 'OK, I'm not sure what's coming up here, but I'm going to stick with what I've been doing and know that it has worked in the past and it's just a matter of time.' That's kind of what we're going through right now."

– Coach Brian Kelly, 2010

"People come to Notre Dame not to learn how to do something, but how to be somebody."

– Lou Holtz

"The only qualifications for a lineman are to be big and dumb. To be a back, you only have to be dumb."

– Knute Rockne

"Confidence comes from execution, execution comes from good practices, good practices come from concentration, and concentration comes from a cause."

– Lou Holtz

"I am often asked whether there is a special spirit at Notre Dame. In 1936 a judge ruled that there is a Santa Claus and a spirit of Christmas. The spirit of Notre Dame is the same kind of thing. The minute you make up your mind to believe in it you feel it."

– Lou Holtz

"It isn't necessary to see a good tackle. You can hear it."

– Knute Rockne

"Everybody is saying that because of all these things, we can't be great. They think because you've paid a price academically and are disciplined and make sacrifices, that you can't be tough... there are people who think Notre Dame can't win anymore. I don't believe that."

– Lou Holtz

It was 1930 and Rockne's team, thus far unde-feated, made its way by train to Los Angeles for a battle with Southern California. The Coliseum was filled with 73,000 fans who saw the Irish win decisively, 27-0. Robert Burns recounts:

"American Catholics, ever-conscious of their minority status in the country, savored these wonderful weeks of sports glory as much or perhaps even more than did the coach, players, and university leaders. Almost in the spirit of a holy day of obligation...Catholics of all degrees of religious attachment showed their apprecia-tion for what the team had done for their pride and self-esteem by turning out en masse at rail-road stations along the route from Los Angeles to Chicago to cheer their heroes homeward.

"The Methodists of the country may have

defeated Al Smith in 1928, but the Methodists of the University of Southern California could not beat Notre Dame.

"When the Notre Dame team arrived in Chicago on December 10, the city fathers, responding to the enthusiasm of that city's large Catholic population, organized a ticker-tape parade through the loop area which had been decorated with blue and gold Notre Dame banners. Thousands of people, both in and out of work, forgot their many personal troubles for a day and lined Michigan Avenue and State Street to applaud the Catholic champions of America and their two Jewish halfbacks. Nothing like this extraordinary public demonstration of ethnic and religious pride in sports achievement would occur ever again in Notre Dame history."

– Notre Dame Historian Robert Burns

"It was in the scoreless tie with Army in 1946, as they tell it, that Bob Livingston missed a tackle permitting Doc Blanchard or Glenn Davis to ramble for a good gain. On the bench John Lujack was emotionally keyed up and shouted: 'Oh, Bob Livingston, you son of a bitch.'

"Coach Leahy turned and said piercingly: 'Another sacrilegious outburst like that, Jonathan Lujack, and you will be disassociated from our fine Catholic University.'

"The very next play, Livingston missed another tackle, and Leahy said to the bench: 'Lads, Jonathan Lujack was right about Robert Livingston.'"

– *Dave Condon, sportswriter,*
in the Chicago Tribune

"Motivation is simple. You eliminate those who are not motivated."

– *Lou Holtz*

"Every sport needs its kings. Kings define excellence and provide a standard for everyone else in the sport to measure themselves against. They are loved and hated, respected and feared, revered and reviled. They are royalty, regardless of the year, regardless of the era. Baseball has the Yankees, pro basketball the Celtics, pro hockey the Canadiens. And college football has Notre Dame."

– *ESPN*

"Like other Notre Dame coaches, before and since, Elmer [Layden] was aware that officials in other areas—particularly on the West Coast—do not always seem to interpret the rules in a consistent fashion.

"And ironically, this 'quiet' man had the courage of his convictions on a December day in the Los Angeles Coliseum. Late in the game with Notre Dame leading, 10-6, Southern California mounted a yard-consuming rally on a slick passing attack.

"Downfield the Trojans marched, but only seconds were left. But with time for a couple plays left, a long pass fell incomplete, only to have an official (from the West Coast) signal interference on Bernie Crimmins, a sophomore fullback who was defending.

"Layden was outraged at what he thought was a bad call and when the game ended—and the Irish won—seconds later he charged across the field, challenged the official and anyone who would listen. He told Coach Howard Jones how bad it was; he pursued his claim against Willis Hunter, the Trojans athletic director; and even protested to Rufus Von Kleinschmidt, the dignified chancellor of USC.

" 'When I had let off enough steam,' Elmer recalled much later, 'I went into the dressing room and told Crimmins, 'that was an awful call, Bernie, but those things happen.'

" 'But Crimmins looked me in the eye and said, 'Coach, I pushed him!' "

– Joe Doyle, sportswriter for the
South Bend Tribune

One can hear Father Morrissey say:

"Athletics …to be sure, is subordinate to morals and the attainments of the mind, but its functions are positive."

"At the cemetery, police fought the crowds which attempted to get a last glimpse of the casket. Men and women pressed around the grave where relatives and friends stood in mourning. Father O'Donnell conducted the simple burial service, and the casket, with its monogram blanket for mantle, was lowered into the grave by six teammates who had played their best for their coach. Rockne was buried as he lived, simply and earnestly, with his men and his friends gathered around him."

– Notre Dame Scholastic

April 1, 2001 – The Savvis Center, St. Louis, MO: It is all on the line for the National Championship in Women's Basketball and it is Notre Dame versus Purdue. The game is tied at 66. Two-time All-American Ruth Riley stood at the free throw line with 5.8 seconds left. Purdue's attempt to ice her with time-outs failed. The two free throws didn't swish, but they were good. Purdue had time for one last shot. Katie Douglas of Purdue took the shot from 17 feet out. It hit the rim and bounced out.

As author Mark Bradford put it:

"Such are the things of a perfect championship. Such are the results of hard work and determination. Such are the things of dreams come true. Notre Dame. National Champions."

Who can forget the Women's NCAA basketball championship team, coached by Muffet McGraw and led by Ruth Riley, Niele Ivey, Alicia Ratay, Erika Haney and Kelley Siemon—or the incredible reception given the Lady Irish as they returned to campus. It was freezing cold and nearly 3 a.m. When they arrived, some 3,000 fans and a brand new national championship team sang together the "Notre Dame Victory March." Sr. Jean Lenz provided these details:

"I had watched other coaches and teams make their way to 'the circle' near the Morris Inn after their big wins: Ara Parseghian, Digger Phelps and Dan Devine. ...But this night was different from the others. Coach Muffet McGraw and her 2001 women's basketball team were about to roll down Notre Dame Avenue in their minibuses with a fully certified national championship, nailed down by co-captain Ruth Riley when she hit the last two winning baskets in the game against Purdue from the free throw line with 5.8 seconds left on the clock. I had to get to this parade on time.

"First estimates of arrival time (announced in Farley Hall, home of senior starter Kelley Siemon) were 1:00 a.m., but it wasn't until after 2:00 when the minibuses finally hit Notre Dame Avenue and Angela Boulevard, causing an outburst of recognition that marked the start of the parade. As the moon moved across the sky, thousands of fans of all ages milled about in the magic of the moment in twenty-degree weather. Many wide-eyed students shivered audibly, wrapped in their bed blankets as the band filled the air with ND favorites, giving playtime to bagpipes along the way. With flashing lights, campus security cars led the entourage to the first platform I had ever seen for such an occasion.

"...Steeped in the thrill of their win, the players made their way to the platform with arms waving and faces filled with captivating smiles. Somewhat stunned, Coach McGraw stood at the center of the uproar with megaphone in hand, declaring breathlessly, 'Nothing like this has ever happened to me before.' I was thinking the same thing as my eyes swept across the clear night sky filled with a bright spring moon and a Golden Dome all ablaze. It was a quintessential ND moment, with a woman's touch."

– Sr. Jean Lenz, O.F.M.

"Coach Holtz would tell us that we would have a half-day practice today. We were all excited until he said it would be a half day, eight in the morning until eight at night."

– Ned Bolcar, Captain of the '88 Irish,
cited by John Heisler

"Winning, of course, is the goal of every coach and team, and the will to win is surely an important part of the Notre Dame spirit. Here athletic programs have always been, clearly and very deliberately, part of a larger educational effort. In their day and in their own ways, Rockne, Leahy and Parseghian were among the preeminent 'professors' on the campus. Rockne taught more than the game of football; he taught a philosophy, a way of looking at life and living its opportunities, misfortunes and challenges. He had once taught science, and although he chose to give up the science, he never gave up being a teacher. He wanted to be a builder of men and of character."

– *Ed "Moose" Krause*

"Moose in the casket is in better shape than any of us."

– *Ara Parseghian commenting on the pallbearers who escorted Ed "Moose" Krause to his final resting place*

"[Ara] joked that Colonel Stephens may have done one of the worst recruiting jobs in school history in assembling the group who carried Krause's casket. Lou Holtz was so slight, he looked like a strong wind could knock him off his feet. George Kelly, Dick Rosenthal, George Connor and Parseghian could barely support themselves on their unsteady legs, much less the weight of Moose and his legend. And the Colonel himself, as his friends often reminded him, was so short his feet didn't touch the ground."

– Jason Kelly

Kevin Coyne described the graveside moment as Edward "Moose" Krause was laid to rest:

"The gentle rain mixed easily with the silent tears that rolled down the cheeks of the singers. The fight song—a sturdy and familiar vessel for their emotions—had coaxed out their grief from the reluctant corners where it often hides in the hearts of men: it gave them a language for their sadness, a memory of their joy. As eternal as the song had always seemed to them, they had reached an age at which they knew they would not be singing it forever. The triumph they were celebrating as they sang now was a triumph beyond the stadium, beyond Notre Dame, a triumph they all hoped to share in one day...

" 'While her loyal sons are marching Onward to Victory.' "

"Coaching burns out a man's insides. It's more than tension—Oh it's far worse."

– Coach Frank Leahy, 1953

"I'd have to say that hiring Ara Parseghian was one of the smartest things we did..."

– Fr. Theodore Hesburgh, C.S.C.

"As I mentioned when I was on your campus last year, Knute liked spirit in his ballplayers. Once when he was working with his four backfield stars who became known as the Four Horsemen, one of them, a fellow named Jim Crowley, just couldn't get it right. You know, I never tell ethnic jokes unless they're about the Irish. But maybe today I can be permitted some leeway. Rockne, who by the way was Norwegian, was commonly called 'the Swede.' He finally got exasperated after Crowley muffed a play, and hollered, 'What's dumber than a dumb Irishman?' Without missing a beat, Crowley said, 'a smart Swede.'"

– President Ronald Reagan to the
1988 Notre Dame National Champions

The following story comes from Mike Collins, long-time voice of Notre Dame Stadium:

"Mistakes will be made and my biggest or at least most infamous occurred in the mid-'80s. We were playing Navy and even though it was early November it was the coldest day ever for me at the Stadium and I have been to every game since 1963. The wind was howling and lake effect snow seemed to be coming down in huge bursts. I found out later the wind chill bottomed out during the game at minus seven degrees. I am sitting on a hard metal stool and the cord to the microphone was not long enough for me even to stand up. I was frozen in place and all I wanted was for the game to end. Most of the fans took matters into their own hands, or in this case, feet, and left. I have never seen fewer fans in Notre Dame Stadium during the fourth quarter than I did that day.

"You might recall that Navy had a terrific running back during that period by the name of Napoleon McCallum. He was a legitimate All-American candidate and to burnish his credentials and with the Naval Academy trailing badly, all they did in the fourth quarter was hand the ball off to McCallum. So with my brain frozen, I just kept repeating on Navy's final drive,

'That's McCallum on the carry for a gain of four' or whatever.

"What I did not notice—remember the snow made it difficult to see across the field—was that, after McCallum was tackled near his own sideline, he went to the bench, probably to save himself from hypothermia. Navy runs the ball on the next play and like a one-trick dog, I just repeated myself, 'That's McCallum on the carry for a gain of two.'

"Lo and behold, some fan directly below my booth yells out at the top of his voice, 'That was Smith, you idiot.' So I'm thinking, 'what does this guy care and why is he so dumb that he's still here?' Anyway, no one I know is still in the stands to hear me called an idiot so forget about it; it's over and I am out of here.

"These were still the days when an edited version of Notre Dame games was played on television the next day. That Sunday I am in my easy chair, still covered in three or four blankets, reading the *South Bend Tribune*, with the replay on television. Yep, you guessed right. As clear as a bell as soon as someone other than McCallum carried the ball, I could hear in the background, 'That was Smith, you idiot.' I just stared at the television, practically frozen in place."

– *Mike Collins*

"We certainly want all our athletic programs to excel, just as we want the bands and the Glee Club and the other choral groups and our student government and the student publications to excel...Thus it is in athletics. We are a place that takes academics seriously, that gives a meaningful degree, that tries to play by the rules and that tries to support our student athletes so that they can have a meaningful experience here. Still, any of us traveling or meeting faculty from elsewhere will invariably find that every other dimension of Notre Dame's excellence is subsumed within the question: 'How's the football team going to be?'"

– Fr. Edward A. Malloy, C.S.C.
(final address to faculty Oct. 5, 2004)

"You can't buy it, you can't wish for it, it just seems to happen. I have been blessed to be around Notre Dame for all of my adult life. In recent years I realized how much the University has become the fabric of my life....It has to do with trying to live your life in a way that would make the University proud....I see it today in the current students. Working on campus a couple of days a week, I have gotten to know dozens of students from all over the world. What a joy it is to hear them talk about doing something good for others with their Notre Dame education.

"I am proud to be the Voice of Notre Dame Stadium but football is a game, life is not. If we can all leave behind a fabric from our lives, because of Notre Dame, it can be said we lived like a champion every day."

– Mike Collins

Sergeant Tim McCarthy, the long-time messenger for sane and sober driving, describes the first time he used a humorous quip to get crowd attention for his fourth-quarter safety plea.

"Remember, the automobile replaced the horse... but the driver should stay on the wagon!"

The reaction from the crowd below:

"was a combination of laughs, groans and boos.... At the next game the message regarded driver attitude, ending with, 'Some drivers are like steel...no good if they lose their temper!' That also went well, including the groans and booing."

Sensing that people were quieting down to hear his messages, McCarthy kept them coming:

"Many of the quips were so corny that the booing increased, particularly from the students. I never thought I would appreciate being booed. It didn't bother me..."

By the third season, the booing gave way to cheers and thus it has been for fifty seasons.
Here are a few of the crowd favorites:

- "Weaving in and out of traffic...can make you a basket case."

• • • • •

- "Following too close...is not the way to make ends meet."

• • • • •

- "Remember, driving half lit...is not very bright."

• • • • •

- "Safe drivers get the cheers...by avoiding the booze."

• • • • •

- "When traffic becomes thick as fleas...don't let it bug you."

• • • • •

- "A sleepy driver...can become a wake."

• • • • •

- "Tearing up the highway...could be the end of the road."

• • • • •

- "The road to court is not a freeway...it is expensive."

• • • • •

- "Remember, alcohol may make you feel exhilarated...but you may not be able to pronounce it."

• • • • •

- "Drive like a musician...C sharp or B flat."

• • • • •

- "If more people drive right...there will be more people left."

"David Ruffer has not forgotten where he comes from. If he did, he wouldn't be able to find his room.

"The nation's most accurate walk-on kicker still lives in Siegfried Hall on Notre Dame's campus, a spot from which the journey to Notre Dame Stadium is more winding than one might think.

"When he can, Ruffer still attends interhall football games, where his implausible story began. He was a high school golfer. He played soccer for one year. He never played football. After transferring to Notre Dame in 2008, he kicked for Siegfried and was plucked for a tryout with the Irish.

"Now, no one in Notre Dame history has made more consecutive field goals than Ruffer. With 11 in a row this year alone, he's at 16 and counting himself astounded. All three members of the kicking operation—including snapper Bill Flavin and holder Ryan Kavanagh—are walk-ons. Asked to describe his expectations of a walk-on kicker, Irish coach Brian Kelly went with 'very low.'

" 'I don't tell him a knock-knock joke on the way out there,' Kavanagh said. 'I try to make sure he's focused on the right things and not stressing about everything. I don't say, 'Hey, if you make this, you're the all-time leading kicker in Notre Dame history, no pressure.' "

– Chicago Tribune *sportswriter Brian Hamilton*

"George Kelly was a successful assistant football coach at Notre Dame for 12 years. He coached under the legendary Ara Parseghian. Kelly coached 13 of his linebackers to the pro level. Later, Kelly moved into administration and continued to care deeply...about anything he could do to make Notre Dame better.

"I used to see him put a chilled diet cola in coach Lou Holtz's car just before Holtz left Notre Dame Stadium after games. Kelly wasn't too big to do that humble act. When the small civic club I belonged to needed a speaker to come to

Honker's Restaurant to deliver a program, Kelly was there. He wasn't too big to come speak in a little room to about 25 people. He cared to third level all 75 of his years."

– Charlie Adams

"It's everybody's story. It's everybody who has obstacles; it's everybody who has dreams."

– Rudy

"On decommitments in recruiting: 'The reality of it today is, there is so much scrutiny relative to the kids in the recruiting process. I've told our staff that unless I see a letter of intent, you need to keep recruiting them. Certainly we would all like to say the value of a person's word is a bond, but there are so many shifting and moving pieces out there that I'm not tripping over that. Would I like somebody to be that guy that says, "That's my word and it's a bond and we're not going to break it"? Certainly. Because we're not going to do it on our end. So I've told our staff, gotta keep recruiting. It's the University of Notre Dame. Nobody's going to give it to you for free.' "

– Coach Brian Kelly, cited by Brian Hamilton

David Casstevens of the *Dallas Morning News* tells a story about Frank Szymanski, a Notre Dame center in the 1940s, who had been called as a witness in a civil suit in South Bend. The judge asked Szymanski:

"Are you on the Notre Dame football team this year?"

"Yes, your Honor."

"What position?"

"Center, your Honor."

"How good a center?"

"Sir, I am the best center Notre Dame has ever had."

Coach Frank Leahy, who was in the courtroom, was surprised. Szymanski had always been modest and unassuming. So, when the proceedings were over, he took Szymanski aside and asked why he had made such a statement. Szymanski blushed and answered:

"I hated to do it, Coach; but, after all, I was under oath."

"I can honestly say that the Notre Dame years were the greatest period of my life and my family's life. Our loyalty to and respect for Notre Dame will always be a part of me."

– *Ara Parseghian*

"Dear Lord:
  In the battle that goes on for life,
  I ask for a field that is fair,
  A chance that is equal with all in strife,
  The courage to do and to dare.

"If I should win, let it be by the code,
  My faith and my honor held high,
  If I should lose, let me stand by the road,
  And cheer as the winner rides by."

  – Attributed to Knute Rockne

"Right now, we have probably 130 students on our campus that would not be here if not for the NBC contract."

  – Fr. William Beauchamp, C.S.C.,
  former Vice-President, Notre Dame

"I shall be very glad to talk for five minutes on the radio about six o'clock, on the way to the Edgewater Beach Hotel. However, the boys on the team are scared to death to talk on the radio, and I wish you would excuse them at this time."

  – Knute Rockne, responding to a request
  from a Chicago radio station

"...(I)n allowing our games to be televised, we have been able to present sidelight stories on the educational, cultural and religious aspects of the University of Notre Dame. And, in itself, this latter has become a point of far greater importance to those guiding the destiny of Notre Dame than the mere televising of an athletic contest."

– Edward "Moose" Krause

"I sometimes wondered if the reporter was at the game. We're beating Purdue 20-0, I'll never forget this, I'm walking off the field at halftime...you know you have to do the interview, your mind's on other things, but it's all part of it. The question was, 'You're only ahead 20-0, are you going to chew your team out?' I remember commenting that the other team gave scholarships too."

– Lou Holtz on halftime interviews

"College football fans either love or hate Notre Dame, and few fall in-between. ...Whether fans root for or against Notre Dame, broadcast ratings speak to the popularity of the Fighting Irish."

– Dick Enberg

A book that aspires to describe Notre Dame through quotations and, sometimes, the stories behind the quotes, must pay homage to the man who was, for decades, synonymous with Notre Dame football, Joe Boland. He was surely the quintessential Notre Dame man.

Notre Dame football on network radio was pioneered by Joe Boland and WSBT. The Irish Football Network debuted in 1947 and, by 1953, the network broadcast games on 115 affiliates in 31 states plus the Armed Forces Network. In 1956 and '57, Notre Dame awarded radio broadcast rights to the Mutual Network and then, for ten years, ND games were carried by the ABC radio network. In 1968, Mutual returned and was succeeded by Westwood One. No other college team had such widespread national coverage. Until his death in 1960, at the age of 55, Joe Boland was the true voice of Notre Dame. Tributes to Joe poured in:

"I felt that Joe underscored the real Notre Dame man—spiritually, intellectually and physically. He was the finest ad conceivable for the University."
– Tim Cohane, Sports Editor, Look *magazine*

• • • • •

"The history of the play-by-play coverage of Notre Dame football is a marvelous success story, both for broadcasters and Notre Dame. It is difficult to comprehend the success of one without the other. One cannot understand the development of American broadcasting, and sports broadcasting specifically, without recognizing the role that Notre Dame played in that history. Similarly, one cannot appreciate the Notre Dame mystique without recognizing the contribution of broadcasters in building that mystique."

– Author Paul Gullifor

• • • • •

"Joe Boland didn't make a million dollars, but he lived his own principles in both his public and private life. He altered the patterns of radio and television reporting for the better, and he made more than a million friends."

– Joe Petritz, then Sports Publicity Director, Notre Dame

• • • • •

"No opposition sportscaster who ever followed us was fairer to us, or better informed about football, or described the game on a higher plane of sportsmanship."

– Bud Wilkinson, University of Oklahoma

• • • • •

"Joe Boland was at least the equal of any football announcer I knew. He had the voice, the articulation, the alert reactions; but he also knew what was going on and he told his audience."

– Author Francis Wallace

• • • • •

"If you couldn't be at a Notre Dame game, the next best thing was to listen to Joe's broadcast of it. Joe, with his wealth of football lore, and his intimate acquaintance with everybody on the field, called the game so realistically you felt you were sitting right next to him. You could almost feel the impact of that tackle. When Joe described a game, you lived that game."

"And his smile! It was a triumph over life's adversities."

"William Busse was the manager of Kreamo Bakery in South Bend in 1930. He was also a flying enthusiast and, by all accounts, one of the great promotional stuntmen of his time, when he hatched the idea of dropping miniature loaves of Kreamo bread by tiny parachutes into Notre Dame Stadium during a nationally-broadcast game. In a 1995 letter to Notre Dame, he described the stunt:

'We filled small boxes with miniature loaves of bread. Back in those days...airplanes did not

fly so fast as they do now. We chose a four-pas-
senger plane, removed the door and loaded it
with one-half-size suit boxes filled with miniature loaves of bread which were stacked from the
floor to the ceiling. I sat in the doorway, with my
feet hanging out, and unloaded the entire load of
half-size men's suit boxes, each containing about
24 miniature loaves wrapped in parachutes. We
had to test the air currents first to see where the
boxes of parachutes would float down. The first
box floated down about two blocks east of the
stadium. The next box came down in the east
stands where the viewers were sitting. We circled
the stadium again and dropped our entire load
so it would float down on the playing field. The
officials had to stop the game and remove the
parachutes and bread so they could continue the
game. This was on national radio throughout
the U.S.A. The following Monday some Notre
Dame executives came to see me and complained
that their football game was interfered with. I
promised that I would never do this again, and I
never have.' "

– Cited by Paul Gullifor

Anyone who ever attended a Notre Dame basketball game in the Fieldhouse will recall how that experience defined "home team advantage." Only about 5,000 people could be shoehorned into the place and, since students attended free of charge, there wasn't much room left for others. The bleachers were so close to the raised court that one could literally reach out and touch a player readying to inbound a pass. In this place, Notre Dame would rise up and smite some of the best teams in the country. Match-ups with Kentucky, Marquette, and DePaul were bound to rock the Fieldhouse. In 1948, legendary coach Adolph Rupp's Kentucky Wildcats, led by Alex Groza, Ralph Beard and Wallace Jones, met Moose Krause's Fighting Irish and the Irish of O'Shea, Barnhorst, and Foley were ready:

"The place, jammed to the rafters with students, became so incredibly loud that Rupp found it impossible to communicate with his team. This 'problem' was amplified by the placement of the Notre Dame band—directly behind the Kentucky bench—and by the presence of some 300-400 members of the Holy Cross community in their black robes—directly across from the Kentucky bench. Following the game [which Notre Dame won 64-55], Rupp claimed that under those circumstances it was impossible to win at Notre Dame, where he was now 0-5, and that he would never bring his Wildcats back as long as he was coach. Unfortunately for the 'Baron,' the ND-UK contract still called for one more visit to the fun house in 1950."

– Historian Tim Neely

(Rupp did come back in 1950 as scheduled, and this time, armed with seven-foot center Bill Spivey; but the Irish won, 64-51. Even before the ACC and Digger Phelps, gamesmanship was part of Notre Dame basketball!)

The Fieldhouse also served as the only indoor place on campus that could hold more than a thousand people. Fr. Hesburgh noted:

"We didn't have a decent place to play, and we were playing more and more teams from the top leagues. It was a disgrace bringing people into what we had. We had Bob Hope out here, and the Fieldhouse was the only place we could get 2,000 people inside. As we finished the program, he said, 'Well, I think it's time to get all you guys out of here and let the cows back in.'"

– Interview with Michael Coffey

In the fall of 1955, Notre Dame's basketball fortunes took a turn for the better with the admission of Tommy Hawkins, only the third black player in Irish history.

"[Tommy] Hawkins would be the second black starter in Notre Dame history and, as with Joe Bertrand, there were questions about how a black man would feel playing for a predominantly white school."

– Michael Coffey

Coffey records the Hawk's own recollection:

"I walked into a downtown South Bend pizza parlor with a date one night. And a guy says to me, 'Do you have reservations?' And I said, 'Reservations? In a pizza parlor? You've got to be kidding.' He said, 'Yeah, you can't come in unless you have reservations.' Well, all of the Notre Dame students there knew what was going down, so they simply discontinued eating and got up and walked out. When the University heard about the situation, the pizza parlor was put off limits to Notre Dame personnel and students until I got a public apology…

"Father Hesburgh, who rates No. 1 on my

list of all-time great men, in a press conference in 1956 when he was asked what he was going to do, said to the nation, 'Anywhere that Tommy Hawkins isn't welcome, Notre Dame isn't welcome.' In the mid-1950s, that statement was huge. That's the kind of backing I got from everybody at Notre Dame."

– Tom Hawkins as told to Michael Coffey

"Hawk's support came from sources other than the university administration. Like Joe Bertrand before him, Hawk was almost unanimously accepted and liked by his classmates—classmates who were not shy about going to bat for their fellow Notre Dame man when the situation required."

– Michael Coffey

"John Jordan loved children. Because of health problems, he and his wife were unable to have children.

"After his wife died, he met a widow from Kalamazoo, and after a period of time they were married. She became pregnant in 1959.

Late in the pregnancy, she fell and broke a hip, and because of her age and the injury, it was a precarious pregnancy. She was very popular with the team, and so there was more than the usual concern you'd naturally feel for a development like that.

"We had a traditional game on New Year's Eve with Northwestern, and Eileen was due at just that time. The team took the bus to Chicago without Coach Jordan, who stayed behind to be with Eileen. We stayed at the Sheraton Hotel on Michigan Avenue and went through the scouting report, pregame meal, got on the bus—still no John Jordan.

"Just as the bus was about to pull away from the curb, a car screeched to a stop ahead of it. Coach Jordan jumps out, leaps up the stairs, and from the front of the bus, with an even more florid Irish face than usual, booms out, 'It's a girl, Bridget Ann!' Wild cheering broke out on the bus.

"We took our usual warm-ups and as we went back to the locker room for the final words before tip-off, Coach Jordan said, 'I've asked you to win one for your parents, I've asked you to win one for Notre Dame, and I've asked you to win one for yourselves. But I've never asked you to win one for me. Let's get out and win this one for Bridget Ann!'

"We left the locker room like troops going over the tops of trenches in a major war. But our enthusiasm didn't quite measure up to our first-half ability, and we came down at halftime losing by 20 or some ridiculous deficit like that.

"Our pep talk consisted of the same florid face appearing briefly behind the open door, screaming, 'You stink,' and slamming the door. We got ourselves all charged up again, determined to make up the deficit and win one for the new Jordan heir. But the final score was 102-67—the worst defeat in Notre Dame history up to that point. In years afterward, when I'd visit with Coach and his family, I had trouble looking little Bridget in the face, and I'm sure the same was true for other members of that team."

— *John Tully (interview with Michael Coffey)*

SPORTS FACT: University of Notre Dame athletic programs rank No. 1 in Graduation rates, based on Graduation Success Rate (GSR) figures released by the NCAA—including first-place ratings in the sports of football, men's basketball and women's basketball, and a close second in ice hockey (2010).

"I'm going to Notre Dame for football, but that's not the only thing I'm going there for. I'm also going for the school and the academics and the history and the tradition. None of that has changed. It's kind of like our [high] school. We had a couple of bad seasons. But we worked really hard and fought our way through it and got better and now we're winning."

– Stephon Tuitt, DE, Monroe, GA

"There is a pressure in every coaching job, but winning makes it a lot easier to accept. Fortunately, we have been winning. But like one fan told me, 'We're with you, Ara, win or tie. You notice he didn't say anything about losing."

– Ara Parseghian

"The great American humorist Will Rogers said at the news of Rockne's death, 'It takes a big calamity to shock this country all at once, but Knute, you did it. You died one of our national heroes. Notre Dame was your address, but every gridiron in America your home.'"

– Robert Quackenbush '76

Jim Crowley, one of the Four Horsemen, re-counted one of Rockne's motivational efforts:

"We were playing Georgia Tech in 1922 and they had been undefeated on their home field for years. Rockne came into the dressing room carrying a telegram. 'I have a wire here, boys, and it probably doesn't mean much to you but it means a great deal to me. It's from my poor, sick little boy Billy who's critically ill in the hospital in South Bend.' And then he read the wire, with teary eyes, a lump in his throat and quivering lips: 'I want Daddy's team to win.'... We took a hell of a pounding from this great Georgia Tech team because they had been out to beat us for years. But we won the game for little Billy, 13-3.

"Well, when we got back to South Bend, there must have been about 20,000 people to greet us. And as we stepped off the train racked with pain, the first face we saw was Rockne's kid. He was in the front line. There was 'poor, sick little Billy' looking like an ad for Pet Milk."

"This is Notre Dame. Next time you score, act like you've been there before."

– Lou Holtz to a young back who had danced in the end zone after a touchdown

232

Edward "Moose" Krause has been the subject of a book, *Mr. Notre Dame*, a moniker that fit him perfectly. Father Hesburgh once said that if he knew a saint at Notre Dame, it was Moose. In his student days, he was a standout tackle on the football team. But basketball was his real forte. A two-time All-American at Notre Dame, Krause was a remarkable mix of talent and a sense of humor. Jason Kelly tells the story:

"In 1933, the Irish were trailing Butler by two points with only seconds remaining in the game. With time running out, Krause missed a shot that could have tied the game; there was a crush of bodies seeking the rebound. Krause landed on the floor. 'There I was, stretched out on the hardwood,' he recalled, 'with players jumping on and off my head as fast as I could count.' Then his own missed shot bounced right back into his arms. Lying on his back, he shot and hit the tying basket and the Irish went on to a 42-41 win in overtime.

"Coach George Keogan kidded Krause, saying that he should shoot from the horizontal position more often. ...Later, in practice, Coach Keogan found his entire team flat on their backs as they rehearsed the Krause shot."

"A team is no stronger than its weakest player on the field or the weakest coach on its staff....We did not necessarily look for coaches who had the deepest technical knowledge of football. What we wanted were quality people of integrity, people who could contribute knowledge and enthusiasm to our joint effort. We found them and they joined us."

– Ara Parseghian

One of Coach Frank Leahy's regular routines was to tell everyone how afraid he was of the next opponent and how he hoped the Irish would be able to compete against such powerful rivals. At one point, he was talking up the next opponent and advised Ziggy Czorobski that the lineman he'd be facing was a great football player and a brilliant student:

"Oh, Zygmont, I don't know how you will ever deal with such a combination of brawn and brain."

To which Ziggy replied:

"Don't worry, Coach, after I hit him a couple of times, he'll be as dumb as I am."

(Actually, Ziggy was no dummy...
but he was a character!)

234

"The original Notre Dame mascot was an Irish terrier. A series of dogs played the role, the first being a dog named "Tipperary Terrence" who was presented to Notre Dame head coach Knute Rockne in 1924. This dog was replaced by "Brick Top Shuan-Rhu," another Irish terrier, in 1930.

"In 1933, Brick Top was replaced by a dog named 'Clashmore Mike,' who proved so popular and beloved that all successor dogs were given the same name.

"Clashmore Mike was a splendid mascot as he could be used to great effect if made to do a series of simple tricks. At half time, for example, the handler would run Clashmore Mike around the stadium and, as he made his rounds, he would stop and lift his leg on the opposing team's bench to howls of delight from the fans.

"For the famous Navy-Notre Dame game, Clashmore Mike's handlers would announce that they had been feeding the dog goat meat all week long. In addition, the dog was trained to chase and attack any goat he came across, so that when the Navy goat-mascot came onto the field leading the Navy team, Clashmore Mike took after him at top speed, again to great howls of laughter and the embarrassment of Navy football fans.

"Clashmore Mike was replaced as the school's mascot in 1965, when the Leprechaun became Notre Dame's official mascot. It was a great step down, in my opinion—from reality to fantasy, and from a dog with character to a mere cartoon."

– *Patrick Burns*

Posted by 2001 Notre Dame women's basketball alum Ruth Riley:

"An entire decade has passed since my teammates and I stood huddled up at Notre Dame's center court, where we reunited this weekend to celebrate our 2001 National Championship. We had an amazing time from being honored at the women's game on Friday, to our team dinner that night where we were able to catch up on each other's lives and joke around about some of the comical experiences we shared, to being honored at the football game on Saturday.

"Since I have been blessed to win a championship in every level, many people ask me which one is the most memorable. I generally say, there is no greater honor than representing your country and winning a gold medal, but the most memorable for me was winning a national championship at Notre Dame. There is just something unique and special about the amateur aspect of college athletics, and then finishing my entire collegiate career on top was simply amazing.

"Prior to the women's game Friday night, Notre Dame took me by complete surprise as they unveiled a banner with my name and number, designating me as the first female athlete to be inducted into the newly established ring of honor around the arena. I was so grateful to have my family and teammates there with me, without them I would have never become the player and person I did and continue to be today!

"As we walked out to be introduced at half-time, I was filled with mixed emotions. I am not a player to spend much time reliving the 'glory days' but it was impossible to escape the flash-backs of the nervousness and anxiety I felt as I stepped onto that court for my very first practice, the sadness of senior night when I realized it was my last home game representing the Fighting Irish, and the various emotions that accompanied all the practices and games in between.

"We were fortunate to have everyone make it back for the weekend, and I could not help but find it ironic that it was not the people, but the place that changed the most. My teammates look exactly the same as when I left them 10 years ago, but it was the arena that I did not recognize. It has been completely renovated with new seats, an added club level as well as the addition of a brand new state-of-the-art jumbotron over mid-court. Looking around, I could not help but be filled with pride, purpose and contentment in knowing that my teammates and I were instru-mental in building the program to the level it is today. Our contribution was not isolated to what we accomplished in 2001, but we could see the tangible effects our careers had. There is something very fulfilling in knowing that not only were we successful, but we, like so many teams before us, have helped script various chapters in the legacy of Notre Dame women's basketball. It was equally exciting to see the current players and know they are not only carrying that on today, but they are continuing to carry it forward!

"Lastly, I was overwhelmed with a sense of gratitude. First to my family for their unwavering love and support over the years! Secondly, to my teammates and the basketball staff for their friendship, guidance, and all the memories we share. To the university, for their investment in our lives as they provided the resources to enable us to be successful on the court and in life. Last, but definitely not least, to the community of South Bend, and the Notre Dame fans everywhere, for the love and support they have shown and continue to show us!!

"GO IRISH!"

FACT: The old Notre Dame Fieldhouse was demolished in March, 1983. The Irish had played basketball there for 63 seasons and, with the help of raucous crowds, won 84% of their games in that venue.

Freshman Adriana Leon scored in the 63rd minute to help the Fighting Irish defeat Stanford 1-0 (2010) for their third NCAA Women's College Cup championship. Melissa Henderson assisted on the goal for Notre Dame (21-2-2), which joined North Carolina as the only schools with at least three Women's College Cup titles.

Irish Coach Randy Waldrum said:

"Please have the courage to write that this was the best team in the country, not that this was an upset. I know everybody had preordained Stanford as the national champion this year. But I would make the argument that once the NCAA tournament started, the path we took and the way we won games...we clearly were the best team in the country."

Notre Dame was ranked No. 2 behind UCLA when the Bruins came to town on January 19, 1974. As Bill Paterno remembers:

"Led by superstar Bill Walton, the Bruins had not lost a game since their visit to South Bend in 1971. They continued to mow down opponent after opponent, and had their win streak up to 88 games when they arrived at the Athletic and Convocation Center, with TVs on hand to bring the game live to the nation.

"Phelps, with his knack for showmanship and preparation, knew exactly how to get the team set psychologically. At the close of practice in the week before the game, he got out ladders and had the team practice cutting down the nets as they would after a monumental victory."

It is sometimes forgotten that the Irish trailed UCLA 70-59 with 3:21 left in the game.

"As the clock wound down, so did the Bruin lead. Shumate scored, then stole the UCLA inbounds pass and scored again. Dantley picked Keith Wilkes's pocket and went the distance for a lay-up. Tommy Curtis was the victim of a questionable traveling call, and Brokaw cut the lead to three with a jumper over Wilkes and to one with another from the free-throw circle.

"With less than a minute remaining, Martin drew a charge on Wilkes, nullifying a basket and giving the Irish the ball and a chance for the win. Needing a last-second shot for a big victory, the Irish turned to the man who had done the job for them so many times before.

"With 29 seconds remaining, [Dwight] Clay's high-arcing shot swished through the net, giving the Irish their first lead of the game, 71-70.

"The Bruins wanted the ball in Walton's hands, and after missed shots by Curtis and

Meyers, they got it. But the normally dead-eyed big man missed only his second shot of the game. Pete Trgovich and Meyers couldn't get putbacks to go before Shumate corralled the rebound. The bedlam in the stands spilled out onto the court. Notre Dame was #1 for the first time since 1949."

– Michael Coffey

"The year was 1964. Joe Kuharich's 1963 Irish had sunk to a 2-7 record and now Ara Parseghian was at the helm. What he did was close to miraculous. With one game left, they had beaten all nine opponents and needed only one more win to claim the National Championship and complete a worst-to-first scenario. The impossible dream was ended by USC in a ferocious battle, 20-17. Ara told his men after the game, 'I want all of you to hold your tongues, to lift your heads high, and in the face of defeat be Notre Dame men. I've never been associated with a greater bunch than you guys. No one will ever forget the achievements you made this year.'

"On the day the team flew back, supporters had lined the streets from the airport to campus, applauding their heroes in 9° temperatures. The team buses headed for the Old Fieldhouse where it seemed half the free world had assembled. The overflow stood outside in the snow.

"The next thirty minutes were as emotional as any this university had ever generated. The crowd erupted when they saw the team enter. The players and coaches were escorted to their seats to a steadily building ovation. The applause and chants lasted for twenty minutes. This was to have been a spontaneous program. Still, Parseghian felt he should address these supporters.

" 'We wanted to bring you back the national championship,' he began.

" 'You did, you did, you did,' they shouted.

"Parseghian could not continue. The band played the Victory March and then the Alma Mater. No one, players and coaches alike, could hold back the tears."

– Bob Best and Tom Pagna

"The moments of splendor, the ruthlessness of injury, the private inner sanctum of one's naked feeling exposed in loss or victory, the humor and tragedy of men at *play* and work can never be captured totally in words or pictures."

– Ara Parseghian

The year was 1973 and the 10-0 Fighting Irish met Bear Bryant's Alabama powerhouse in the Sugar Bowl with the Championship on the line. It was a mythic struggle. Late in the game, Ara called on Bob Thomas for a 32-yard field goal attempt. It barely made it and put the Irish up 24-23. Ara asked Thomas about the kick when he returned to the bench. Thomas quipped:

"I was thinking on the way out that if I stuck it right down the pipe, nobody would ever remember it. This way, they'll be talking about it for years."

– Quoted by Bob Best

The year was 1980. It was late February and the undefeated and number-1-ranked Marquette was coming to the A.C.C. The Irish crowd showed up early and ready to cheer for their team. The chant "25 and 1" was deafening.

Tim Andree remembers:

"The thing that was great about Notre Dame was you were going to school with such great people. The guys on the team were just tremendous men. I remember being upset before that game because I was playing on the blue squad in practice and I knew I wasn't going to get much playing time.

I had said to Gil Salinas before the game that maybe coming to Notre Dame was a mistake and that I couldn't remember why I'd come there. In the warm-up, with the place going crazy and things very exciting, Gil ran by me and yelled in my ear, 'This is why you're here.' "

The Irish won in double overtime.

Think about it: Within a few seasons, the Irish had defeated UCLA with Bill Walton, San Francisco with Bill Cartwright, and Virginia with Ralph Sampson!

January 1, 1979... On the icy, frozen tundra of The Cotton Bowl, with Houston leading 34-12 with just over four minutes remaining in the third quarter, the comeback kid, Joe Montana, fighting the flu, leads the Irish to one of the most thrilling victories in Notre Dame history, 35-34.

"Coach Devine commented on his quarterback who once again had done the seemingly impossible. 'What makes him the leader he is? You saw it today. He proved it to me in the third game of his sophomore year. On our depth charts he was listed last, behind even the walk-ons. That's why Montana is as good as he is. He never quits.'"

– Jeff Jeffers

There are special bonds between players and coaches at every school. At Notre Dame they seem to shine in every sport and coach. My father, Walter Langford, was tennis coach and fencing coach at Notre Dame in addition to teaching full time at the University. His tennis teams won 95, lost 30 and tied 1. More importantly, he insisted that his athletes conduct themselves as true Notre Dame men. And, in return, he made certain that they were given every chance to succeed.

Coach Tom Fallon's book, *The Story of Notre Dame Tennis*, recounts this story, told by Phil Lyons, a walk-on player in 1947:

" 'I was a walk-on player from New Mexico and a graduate of a high school that had no tennis program. Here I was playing on a team that had just unbelievably skilled players. When the final meet of the season rolled around...I needed just one more victory to earn my monogram, but

I had just about abandoned any hope of getting that coveted award, because the road trip limit was seven or eight players and I had very little chance of ousting anyone from the road roster.

" 'Out of nowhere, Coach Langford told me to pack my gear for the trip because Joe Brown and Jim Rodgers had volunteered to remain behind just to give me a chance at my monogram. I was stunned at the thoughtfulness of those fellows, but it was the kind of love that was ever present on that team.

"Lyons was inserted into the number-six singles spot by Langford, who in turn proceeded to divide his attention among all six singles matches.

" 'Every time the coach would glance my way, I was struggling. But I was winning the big points. It was a hard-fought match and I won, 6-3, 6-4. I felt great because I had won for my teammates and had locked up my monogram.

" 'After the match, Coach Langford came up to me and said he was going to enter me in the number three doubles with Bill Tully because with Bill as my partner, I was guaranteed a win and my monogram. When I told him I had won my singles match, he was just about flabbergasted. He smiled, congratulated me, and said that Bob David and Ed Caparo would play the final doubles match. I'll never forget his love for his players or the players' love for Coach Langford and each other.' "

"I feel very loyal to Notre Dame. I love this institution and what it stands for. When I first arrived here, I had a lot of growing to do as a coach. Notre Dame helped me through those years, and we're finally reaping the benefits of that. They stood by me while I was gaining experience, and now that I have that, I feel a need to give back to Notre Dame."

– Coach Muffet McGraw

A story that exemplifies the heart of the Notre Dame spirit comes from the 1973 Ara-Parseghian-led Fighting Irish. Having completed a 10-0-0 regular season, the number-one-ranked Irish faced Bear Bryant's number-two-ranked Alabama Crimson Tide in the Sugar Bowl. As expected, it was a classic battle, climaxed by one of the most dramatic plays in Notre Dame football history. With Notre Dame leading 24-23 in the waning moments of the battle,

Alabama punted to the Irish one-yard line. Two running plays moved the ball to the five. Tom Pagna recounts the rest of the story:

"Then on third and six, Ara had his day of reckoning. Alabama stopped the clock with 2:12 left, giving Clements a chance to come to the sideline.

" 'I know it's risky, but let's go with a long cadence,' I suggested.

" 'Great idea,' he replied: 'Tom, take a long count and set up a run-action pass to Casper.'

"For the first time ever, Clements displayed an emotion—surprise. He nodded, though, and ran back on the field. 'Are you sure that's what you want to do, Ara?' I asked. 'Did I hear you right?'

" 'Hell yes you did,' he snapped. 'It's a good call. If they jump, we'll get an easy five yards. If they don't then the rush shouldn't be much and we ought to be able to get the ball away.'

"The teams were at the line of scrimmage now, and I was praying Alabama would jump. A fumble, an interception, a safety—all those were very real possibilities in a passing situation at the five, and any one of them would mean the game. My angle was blocked, but I heard someone shout, 'Damn it! Casper moved too soon!' That cost us half the distance to the goal and pushed us back to the two. Clements looked toward Ara who signaled for the same play.

"Casper was our intended receiver, but Ara had inserted a second tight end, Robin Weber, to disguise our pass plans. With the snap the Alabama secondary converged on Casper, leaving Weber virtually free. He was running a deep pattern toward the Alabama sideline. Meanwhile in the end zone, Clements was fortunate to get the pass off. Two of our players had missed blocks, and an Alabama tackle who should have been on the ground by now lunged toward Tom and barely missed his pass. Weber did some stretching of his own, and after juggling the ball momentarily, he cradled it for his first Notre Dame reception—a 35-yard gain. Now we had breathing room, and with an additional first down we ran out the clock....

" 'The pass from Clements to Weber with seconds to go was the key to the win,' Ara explained to the media. 'It was a win or punt situation. If we hadn't made the first down, Alabama would surely have been in field goal position with us punting from our end zone. I definitely feel we are National Champions.' "

He was right!

Four Horsemen – circa 1924

ANNOTATED
BIBLIOGRAPHY

Ayo, Nicholas, C.S.C. Father Ayo is one of Notre Dame's most profound and yet accessible spiritual writers ever.

– *The Heart of Notre Dame: Spiritual Reflections for Students, Parents, Alumni and Friends* (Notre Dame, IN: Corby Books, 2010). This reads like a portable Notre Dame retreat, with graceful reminders of what in life really matters.

– *Times of Grace: Spiritual Rhythms of the Year at the University of Notre Dame* (Lanham, MD: Rowman and Littlefield, 2004).

- *Signs of Grace: Meditations on the Notre Dame Campus* (Lanham, MD: Rowman and Little-field, 2001).

Bilinski, Bill. *Champions: Lou Holtz's Fighting Irish* [Foreword and Afterword by Lou Holtz] (Notre Dame, IN: Corby Books, 2010). As beat reporter for the *South Bend Tribune*, Bilinski was close to the program. His is the best book on the Holtz era at Notre Dame.

Bradford, Mark. *Nice Girls Finish First: The Remarkable Story of Notre Dame's Rise to the Top of Women's College Basketball* (South Bend, IN: Diamond Communications, 2001).

Branfield, Jerry. *Rockne: The Coach, The Man, The Legend* (Lincoln: University of Nebraska Press, 2009).

Burns, Robert E. *Being Catholic, Being American: The Notre Dame Story, 1842-1934* (Notre Dame, IN: University of Notre Dame Press, 1999); (*volume two, 1934-1952*, 2000). An interesting, well-researched history of Notre Dame from its founding to the aftermath of WWII.

Burrell, David B., C.S.C. *When Faith and Reason Meet: The Legacy of John Zahm, C.S.C.* [With historical sketch by Ralph Weber] (Notre Dame, IN: Corby Books, 2009). A study of the man who steered Notre Dame on the path to academic achievement. Essential reading to understand the history of Notre Dame.

Cashore, Matt, and Kerry Temple. *Celebrating Notre Dame* (Notre Dame, IN: Corby Books, 2007). A full-color portrait of the campus: photos by Cashore, text by Temple.

Coffey, Michael. *Echoes on the Hardwood: One Hundred Seasons of Notre Dame Men's Basketball* (Lanham, MD: Taylor Trade Publishing, 2004). A remarkably good book. Coffey builds a fascinating account of men's basketball at Notre Dame by telling the story in the words of former Irish players, coaches, administrators and observers. He weaves the interviews together in a way that brings the history alive.

Collins, Mike and Tim McCarthy. *May I Have Your Attention Please: Wit and Wisdom from the Notre Dame Press Box* (Notre Dame: Corby Books,

2009). Delightful behind-the-scenes stories from the Press Box, including the best of Sgt. McCarthy's quips about safe driving.

Condon, Dave, Chet Grant and Bob Best. *Notre Dame Football: The Golden Tradition* (South Bend, IN: Icarus Press, 1978).

Connor, Jack. *Leahy's Lads: The Story of the Famous Notre Dame Football Teams of the 1940s.* (South Bend, IN: Diamond Communications, 1994). Jack Connor and his brother, George, played for Frank Leahy during his years of unparalleled success. Easily the best book ever written on Leahy and his Lads.

Corby, William, C.S.C. *Memoirs of Chaplain Life: Three Years with the Irish Brigade in the Army of the Potomac* (New York: Fordham University Press, 1992).

Coyne, Kevin. *Domers: A Year at Notre Dame* (New York: Viking Penguin, 1995). Kevin Coyne spent a year at Notre Dame observing and inter-acting with students, faculty and administrators. His account of that experience is captivating.

Dowling, Mary Pat. *Grotto Stories: from the Heart of Notre Dame* (South Bend, IN: Mary Sunshine Books, 1996).

Ellis, John Tracy. *American Catholics and the Intellectual Life* (Chicago: Heritage Foundation, 1956).

Fallon, Tom. *What Though the Odds....:The Story of Notre Dame Tennis* (South Bend, IN: Diamond Communications, 1994).

Faust, Gerry, John Heisler and Bob Logan. *Gerry Faust's Tales from the Notre Dame Sideline* (Champaign, IL: Sports Publishing, 2004).

– *The Golden Dream* (Champaign: Sports Publishing, 2002).

Fischer, Edward. *Notre Dame Remembered: An Autobiography* (Notre Dame, IN: University of Notre Dame Press, 1987). Ed Fischer was a long-time member of the American Studies Department at Notre Dame, as well as a very perceptive observer of all things Notre Dame.

Gawrych, Andrew, C.S.C. and Kevin Grove, C.S.C. *The Cross Our Only Hope: Daily Reflections in the Holy Cross Tradition* (Notre Dame, IN: Ave Maria Press, 2008).

Grant, Chet. *Before Rockne at Notre Dame* (South Bend, IN: Icarus Press, 1978).

Griffin, Robert, C.S.C. *In the Kingdom of the Lonely God* (Lanham, MD: Sheed and Ward, 2003). Father Griffin was a long-time Director of Campus Ministry at Notre Dame. His writings are always striking.

Gullifor, Paul F. *The Fighting Irish on the Air: The History of Notre Dame Football Broadcasting* (South Bend, IN: Diamond Communications, 2001). A fascinating account of the evolution of radio and television broadcasting of Notre Dame football games. This is enjoyable and informative reading.

Heft, James L. *Faith and the Intellectual Life* (Notre Dame, IN: University of Notre Dame Press, 1996).

Heisler, John. *Greatest Moments in Notre Dame Football* (Chicago: Triumph, 2008).

– *Then Ara Said to Joe* (Chicago: Triumph, 2007).

– *Quotable Rockne* (Nashville: TowleHouse Publishing, 2001).

– *The Notre Dame Football Vault* (Atlanta: Whitman Publishing, 2008).

Hesburgh, Theodore M., C.S.C. [with Jerry Reedy]. *God, Country, Notre Dame* (New York: Doubleday, 1990).

– [as Editor] *The Challenge and Promise of a Catholic University* (Notre Dame: University of Notre Dame Press, 1994).

– *The Hesburgh Papers: Higher Values in Higher Education* (Kansas City: Andrews and McMeel, 1979).

Holtz, Lou [with John Heisler]. *The Fighting Spirit: A Championship Season at Notre Dame* (New York: Pocket Books, 1989).

– *Wins, Losses and Lessons* (New York: Wm. Morrow, 1996).

Hope, Arthur J., C.S.C. *Notre Dame One Hundred Years* (Notre Dame, IN: University of Notre Dame Press, 1948). An informative, delightful read.

Howard, George S. [as Editor] *For the Love of Teaching* (Notre Dame, IN: Academic Publications, 2004).

Hubbard, Donald J. and Mark O. Hubbard. *Forgotten Four: Notre Dame's Greatest Backfield and the 1953 Undefeated Season* (Notre Dame: Corby Books, 2009). The story of Frank Leahy's final team and their incredible undefeated season against one of the toughest schedules in collegiate football history.

Jeffers, Jeff. *Rally! The 12 Greatest Notre Dame Football Comebacks* (South Bend: Icarus Press, 1981).

King, James, C.S.C. *Known by Name: Inside the Halls of Notre Dame* (Notre Dame: Corby Books, 2008). Written by the then Rector of Sorin Hall, this is a real inside view of residence hall life at Notre Dame.

Kelly, Jason. *Mr. Notre Dame: The Life and Legend of Edward "Moose" Krause* (South Bend: Diamond Communications, 2002). A very well-written biography of one of the greatest men in Notre Dame history.

Kessler, Bob. *Things Notre Dame Students Like* (Notre Dame, IN: Corby Books, 2010). This is a very popular, often humorous look at Notre Dame students, what they like and why.

Langford, Jim [and Jeremy Langford]. *The Spirit of Notre Dame: Legends, Traditions and Inspiration from One of America's Most Beloved Universities* (New York: Doubleday, 2005); (New York: Crossroad, 2008).

– [as Editor] *Walking with God in a Fragile World* (Lanham, MD: Rowman and Littlefield, 2003). Contains a wonderful autobiographical chapter by Father Hesburgh and a stirring essay by Notre Dame Theologian Fr. Virgil Elizondo.

Lenz, Jean, O.S.F. *Loyal Sons and Daughters: A Notre Dame Memoir* (Lanham, MD: Rowman and Littlefield, 2002). A delightful recounting of the early years of women at Notre Dame.

Layden, Elmer. *It Was a Different Game* (Englewood Cliffs, NJ: Prentice Hall, 1969).

Maggio, Frank P. *Notre Dame and the Game That Changed Football* (New York: Carroll and Graf, 2007).

Malloy, Edward A., C.S.C. *Monk's Reflections* (Kansas City: Andrews and McMeel, 2003).

– *Culture and Commitment: The Challenges of Today's University* (Notre Dame: University of Notre Dame Press, 1992).

McGraw, Muffet [with Paul Gullifor]. *Courting Success* (Lanham, MD: Taylor Trade, 2003).

Mandell, Ted. *Heart Stoppers and Hail Marys: 100 of the Greatest College Finishes (1970-1999)* (South Bend: Diamond Communications, 2000). If you love college football, this book is for you.

Text is accompanied by a disk with the actual recordings of the winning plays. Seven of the games involve Notre Dame.

Meaney, John W. *O'Malley of Notre Dame* (Notre Dame, IN: University of Notre Dame Press, 1991).

Miscamble, Wilson D., C.S.C. *Go Forth and Do Good: Memorable Notre Dame Commencement Addresses* (Notre Dame, IN: University of Notre Dame Press, 2003).

Murphy, T. L. *Kelly's Heroes: The Irish Brigade at Gettysburg* (Gettysburg, PA: Farnsworth House, 1997).

Neeley, Tim. *Hooping It Up: The Complete History of Notre Dame Basketball* (South Bend, IN: Diamond Communications, 1985).

O'Brien, Michael. *Hesburgh: A Biography* (Washington: Catholic University of America Press, 1998).

O'Connell, Marvin R. *Edward Sorin* (Notre Dame, IN: University of Notre Dame Press, 2001). The definitive biography of the founder of Notre Dame.

Pagna, Tom [with Bob Best]. *Notre Dame's Era of Ara* (South Bend, IN: Diamond Communications, 1994). By far, still the best book on the rebuilding of Notre Dame football under Ara Parseghian.

Poorman, Mark, C.S.C. [Editor] *Labors from the Heart: Mission and Ministry in a Catholic University* (Notre Dame, IN: University of Notre Dame Press, 1996). A remarkably good book of essays by Notre Dame people on the values of a Catholic higher education.

Rockne, Knute. *The Four Winners* (New York: Devin-Adair, 1946).

Schlereth, Thomas J. *The University of Notre Dame: A Portrait of Its History and Campus* (Notre Dame: University of Notre Dame Press, 1991). A valuable tool for understanding the history of the University.

Schmidt, James M. *Notre Dame and the Civil War: Marching Onward to Victory* (Charleston, SC: The History Press, 2010).

Schmuhl, Robert P. *University of Notre Dame: A Contemporary Portrait* (Notre Dame, IN: University of Notre Dame Press, 1986). An indispensable survey of Notre Dame in the process of achieving academic excellence.

Sperber, Murray. *Shake Down the Thunder: The Creation of Notre Dame Football* (New York: Henry Holt, 1993).

Steele, Michael R. *Knute Rockne: A Bio-Bibliography* (Westport, CT.: Greenwood Press, 1983).

Stevens, Christopher. *Fighting to Give: The Jimmy Colveyhouse Story* (Seattle: BookSurge, 2009).

Toohey, William, C.S.C. One of the greatest preachers in the history of Notre Dame, Father Toohey was Director of Campus Ministry at the time of his untimely death. He left behind a legacy in the form of books he had written. Here are a few:

- *A Passion for the Possible* (Notre Dame, IN: Ave Maria Press, 1972).
- *Free at Last: The Christian Odyssey* (Notre Dame, IN: Ave Maria Press, 1970).

- *Fully Alive: Decisions for an Integrated Christian Life* (St. Meinrad, IN: Abbey Press, 1976).

- *Life After Birth: Spirituality for College Students* (New York: Seabury Press, 1980).

Tucker, Todd. *Notre Dame Game Day: Getting There, Getting in, and Getting in the Spirit* (South Bend, IN: Diamond Communications, 2000).

- *Notre Dame vs. The Klan: How the Fighting Irish Defeated the Ku Klux Klan* (Chicago: Loyola Press, 2004).

Twombley, Wells. *Shake Down the Thunder: The Official Biography of Notre Dame's Frank Leahy* (New York: Chilton, 1974).

Ward, Maisie. *Gilbert Keith Chesterton* (Lanham, MD: Sheed and Ward, 2006).